At Home with God

At Home with God

A Complete Liturgical Guide for the Christian Home

GAVIN LONG

PARACLETE PRESS
BREWSTER, MASSACHUSETTS

At Home with God: A Complete Liturgical Guide for the Christian Home

Copyright © 2011 by Gavin Long

ISBN 978-1-55725-685-0

Unless otherwise noted, Scripture quotations are from The Holy Bible, English Standard Version, copyright © 2001 Crossway Bibles, a division of Good News Publishers. Used by permission. All rights reserved.

Scripture quotations marked (NIV) are taken from the Holy Bible, New International Version®, NIV®. Copyright © 1973, 1978, 1984 by Biblica, Inc.™ Used by permission of Zondervan. All rights reserved worldwide.

Scripture quotations marked (NASB) are taken from the NEW AMERICAN STANDARD BIBLE®, Copyright © 1960, 1962, 1963, 1968, 1971, 1972, 1973, 1975, 1977, 1995 by The Lockman Foundation. Used by permission.

Scripture quotations marked (NLT) are taken from the Holy Bible, New Living Translation, copyright © 1996, 2004. Used by permission of Tyndale House Publisher, Inc., Wheaton, Illinois 60189. All rights reserved.

Library of Congress Cataloging-in-Publication Data
Long, Gavin.
  At home with God : a complete liturgical guide for the Christian home /
Gavin Long.
    p. cm.
  ISBN 978-1-55725-685-0
  1. Families—Prayers and devotions. 2. Church year—Prayers and devotions.
I. Title.
  BX2170.F3L66 2011
  249—dc22   2010041990

10 9 8 7 6 5 4 3 2 1

All rights reserved. No portion of this book may be reproduced, stored in an electronic retrieval system, or transmitted in any form or by any means—electronic, mechanical, photocopy, recording, or any other—except for brief quotations in printed reviews, without the prior permission of the publisher.

Published by Paraclete Press
Brewster, Massachusetts
www.paracletepress.com

Printed in Italy

The cross image on the cover of this book is reproduced courtesy of Liguori Publications.

Contents

Introduction

Living a Liturgical Life

Simple home and community rhythms can radically transform our lives. Even though they may be simple, home liturgies reshape the way we see God and the way we see the world around us. They help restore us to the life for which we were created, gently redirecting our thoughts and actions so that we may see the world through God's eyes.

Living in the rhythms of the faith not only helps us navigate our own relation to the world, but it also restores us to each other. Our busy schedules often lead to fragmented existences. Our work identities are different from our social identities, which are also different from our worship identities, which are again different from our home identities. A liturgical life seeks to integrate those disparate identities within the truth of the gospel. This liturgical life fully acknowledges a complete dependence upon God, his presence, and his leadership, where our brokenness begins to give way to wholeness. From our confession that we are entirely dependent upon God for everything, we begin to see our lives, circumstances, relationships, and experiences as gifts from God.

For many, liturgy represents a more formal approach to worship. For others, liturgy is something with which they are comfortable, but largely within the context of corporate worship. For this book, the word *liturgy* has a more expansive definition. Quite simply, a liturgical worldview uses simple reminders to reposition each of us within God's redemptive story. These simple liturgies in our everyday lives reconfirm that we are not the main character of our lives, but rather that God is the center of reality—both the greater cosmic reality and the reality of our lives every day. A liturgical life celebrates the reality that the infinite God who spoke Creation into existence, who holds the world in the palm of his hand, is the same God who knows the number of hairs on our heads. The reality of God's redemptive story for the universe is wrapped up in the details of our everyday lives.

The worldview of the gospel, as we experience it through daily acts within the liturgical life, witnesses God at work around us everywhere and encourages us to lovingly submit to him and, in response, to each other. Daily rhythms of liturgical living shape the way we function. Reminders during the course of the day provide us with invitations to engage or reengage God and each other. The truth of the gospel, then, becomes a beautiful gift—it provides us the lens of the redemptive story that empowers us to see, inquire, and create so that we might be able to navigate the difficulties, complexities, and realities of everyday life.

Creativity and Catholicity

Celebrating the redemptive story in our homes requires a balance of creativity and catholicity. Home and community rhythms are not magic. Rather, their goal is to create an environment for a continuing conversation with God and each other. As you begin to incorporate these liturgical rhythms at home, resist structuralism and uniformity. Embrace learning from each other and adapting expressions that awaken the creativity of your own home and community. Be aware of each other's unique interests and creative gifts. Some may respond to these liturgies and home celebrations with a desire to incorporate more music. Others may respond with a longing to employ more visual arts or food. Recognizing and encouraging each other in those creative responses is essential in the discovery and celebration of our life in God.

Though the value of creativity cannot be overstated, we must also remember that we do not just celebrate any old story. We celebrate the redemptive story that takes us back to the beginning of time to the God who lovingly created the world. God has continued to reveal his love and his redemptive plan throughout history and remains in the process of saving and restoring the world today. To tell such a great story as it deserves to be told, we must include the major branches of the family tree of our faith. For this reason, this book of liturgies and celebrations is inspired by and incorporates aspects of the Hebrew, Eastern Orthodox, Roman Catholic, and Protestant traditions. These home rhythms have been adapted from ancient home and community celebrations, many of which date back thousands of years and are rich in meaning and tradition. The project seeks to recontextualize these celebrations in a meaningful, accessible, and honorable fashion. Respecting and reinvigorating our heritage embraces the historical and theological continuity of the faith while also liberating our creative energies to adapt God's story into today's contexts.

The Journey of the Liturgical Life

I hope these liturgies will awaken new possibilities for families and communities. What I believe you will discover, as my family and community have experienced, is that living *in* and experiencing God's story through these liturgies is more powerful and more transformative than any amount of knowledge we can gather *about* God.

This book is intended to get you started. Discovering your own home traditions is a journey that is full of surprises. You will discover that life in the redemptive story unlocks a sense of creativity and new identity in home and community life. Just remember, the kingdom of God is like a mustard seed. Small steps of faith may begin humbly, but will blossom into fuller, richer expressions as you, your family, and your community walk with God every day.

Home Liturgies for the Liturgical Life

*T*he three basic liturgies for this book are these:
Weekend Sabbath (an entire day of rest)
Weekday prayer and worship
Seasonal home gatherings

Weekend Sabbath

Families may want to prepare for the Sabbath on Saturday—cleaning the home and/or preparing the Sabbath meal together. The opening Sabbath liturgy is intended to be celebrated on Saturday evening and followed by a nice dinner, preferably the most intentional and meaningful dinner of the week. The closing of Sabbath is observed on Sunday evening and is also followed by a meal. From opening to closing, the Sabbath time is set aside for resting, playing, reading, and creating. The Sabbath is designed to be a day of peace and rest where everything "is as it should be."

The Sabbath liturgies carry the themes of each season and introduce the major biblical narratives and church liturgical themes to be celebrated in each week and ultimately throughout the year. Lastly, Sabbaths are excellent opportunities to enjoy life as a family or group and share life with others. These celebrations create an environment where friends can come together and experience the love of Jesus Christ.

OPENING SABBATH

The opening Sabbath liturgy includes the following items:
One large pillar candle[1]
A special cup and wine or grape juice[2]
A special loaf of bread[3]
A dish of olive oil

Within the liturgy, families may choose to insert two songs. The first song is a song of blessing taken from the book of Numbers, chapter 6. The song may be read or the tune may be accessed or downloaded at the athomewithgod.org website. Toward the end of the liturgy, we sing a song of praise that varies from season to season. (Resources and additional ideas for the Sabbath liturgy and the songs for each season may be found at the athomewithgod.org website.)

CLOSING SABBATH

The closing Sabbath liturgy includes the following items:

Two taper candles with candlesticks
A special cup placed in a dish
Wine or grape juice
Incense

The closing Sabbath liturgy can also include a song. Families may choose a song of celebration that connects to the theme of the season. Again, songs and additional resources may be found at the athomewithgod.org website.

Weekday Prayer and Worship

Weekday prayer and worship are extensions of the Sabbath into the week. These liturgies develop further the biblical narratives introduced on the weekend. If appropriate, after this time, believers may wish to retire or disengage from the laboring activities of the day.

Seasonal Home Gatherings

Home gatherings are special invitations to welcome others to celebrate the gospel together. First, these home gatherings are intended to be shared with other believers. In addition, these gatherings are wonderful venues to welcome those outside the immediate community into the loving relationship that believers have with each other. Historically, gatherings like this have also been used to invite and serve those who are struggling, are facing difficulty, or have been marginalized.

Home gatherings are seasonal and celebrate major redemptive themes of the Christian faith:

WINTER—the incarnation of God in Jesus Christ
SPRING—redemption from bondage and new life
SUMMER—the indwelling presence of God
AUTUMN—the journey of faith

These home gatherings are designed to host just a few additional families or individuals, but may be adapted for larger, festival-like environments. The basic home liturgies mentioned above seek to connect the seasons of the Western world with the church liturgical calendar. Therefore, the organization of this book embeds the liturgical calendar within the four seasons.

Scripture References

All Scripture quotations, unless otherwise indicated, are taken from the Holy Bible, English Standard Version. In most instances, an introductory phrase is provided for the reader to establish context or to integrate the Scripture into the larger biblical or seasonal theme.

At Home with God Website
(www.athomewithgod.org)

The website athomewithgod.org has been established to provide you with additional resources—music, recipes, visual media, and access to physical resources. At this site, you can also find additional ideas and explanations around the seasons and the liturgies. The website also serves as a place for you to share liturgical practices and approaches—what works and what does not work—with other readers. Finally, you can receive information on dates and seasonal reminders throughout the year by e-mail upon registering at the website. Throughout the book, this symbol ✚ indicates that additional resources may be found at the athomewithgod.org website.

Preparing for the Season ✳ 15

✠ *This symbol denotes that additional resources or reminders may be found at the athomewithgod.org website.*

Preparing for the Season

$\mathcal{W}inter$ in the Northern Hemisphere ushers in one of the richest and most evocative seasons of the Christian year. It contains three main elements of the redemptive story, each of which focuses on Jesus' coming and God's desire to dwell among us in flesh and blood. The three focal times of winter are:

ADVENT—anticipating the coming of Jesus the King

CHRISTMAS—celebrating Jesus the King's arrival

EPIPHANY—enjoying Jesus the King's life among us

Following these three main periods, the home liturgies shift to a period called Ordinary Time, which simply means "through the year." The final time of winter is this:

WINTER ORDINARY TIME TO ASH WEDNESDAY

Advent

Advent begins the home worship calendar for the year. It anticipates the coming of Jesus Christ as the fullness of God, the fulfillment of all God's promises. References to "Jesus' coming" during this season have a double meaning; they refer to both Jesus' First Coming (his birth) and his Second Coming (his return). Overall, the tone of the season is that of preparation, looking forward to the fulfillment of the promises realized in his birth and return. For dates for Advent for each year, see Appendix B on page 239 or reference the athomewithgod.org website.

Christmas ✚

Christmas is the time that celebrates the fulfillment of God's promises in Jesus Christ. Of course, Christmas Day is observed on December 25 and is set apart to celebrate the birth of Jesus. Throughout much of church history, however, the Twelve Days of Christmas were celebrated to connect Christmas to Epiphany (a historic feast day that celebrates the fullness of the revelation of God in human form through Jesus Christ) and to the beginning of the New Year. You may want to extend your family's Christmas celebration into the New Year by observing the Twelve Days of Christmas.

Epiphany

Epiphany always falls on January 6, which marks the end of the Twelve Days of Christmas. The next four weeks then continue the theme of Epiphany, which centers on the incarnation of God in Jesus Christ. More specifically, Epiphany begins with Jesus' baptism, which marks the beginning of his ministry. During this season, we host a home gathering called *The Celebration of the King*, which celebrates Jesus' life, teachings, and ministry. You may wish to celebrate this home gathering on the weekend of or the weekend immediately following Epiphany.[4]

Winter Ordinary Time to Ash Wednesday

The first weekend of February usually begins Winter Ordinary Time. Depending on the liturgical calendar, it may fall as late as February 9. See the table in Appendix B on page 239 or the athomewithgod.org website for exact dates for each year. This time continues to focus on the life, teachings, and ministry of Jesus while here on earth. This time of the year varies in length because Easter and Ash Wednesday occur at different times each year.

Traditions for the Season

SPECIAL ACTIVITIES

THE ADVENT WREATH AND CANDLES The Advent wreath and candles are the primary symbols used during this season. The church traditionally uses the wreath and candles to tell the redemptive story, beginning with the prophecies of the patriarchs, ranging through the prophets, John the Baptist, and finally, Mary the Mother of God. Ultimately, the candles lead to the celebration of the birth of Christ, the culmination of all these events. The largest candle, which sits in the middle of the wreath, is the Christ candle and is the focal symbol of the Advent wreath. The Christ candle is lit on Christmas Day and may be used throughout the Christmas and Epiphany seasons. Advent liturgies are included within the first four Sabbath liturgies beginning on page 19.

JESSE TREE OR JESSE TREE PROJECT ✠ Another special activity for this season is the Jesse tree or the Jesse tree project.[5] Like the Advent wreath and candles, the Jesse tree tells the redemptive story fulfilled in Jesus. This activity, however, is more involved with its use of symbols. The idea of the Jesse tree comes from Isaiah 11, stating that a branch will come from Jesse's stump. The Jesse tree recounts the entire redemptive story from creation to final restoration, fully realized in Jesus Christ, the fullness of God.

Families or home groups can make ornaments for the Jesse tree. Alternatively, families may want to make crafts, incorporate activities, or paint the symbols on canvas instead of decorating a separate tree. In addition, these symbols may be employed for seasonal home decorations or special decorations for the home gathering of *The Celebration of the King*.

HOME BLESSINGS Historically, the Eastern Orthodox Church has designated the first of the year as a time for blessing each other's homes. This is a time when families gather together, pray for each other, and seek God's blessings for the new year ahead. A liturgy for home blessing is located in Appendix D on page 241.

SPECIAL SYMBOLS FOR THE SEASON

Families or home groups may want to incorporate colors, foods, or other symbols to bring a warmer, more sensory experience to celebrating each season. Below is a list of signs and symbols that could be used for these seasons.

PURPLE OR ROYAL BLUE FOR ADVENT In this season, many churches use purple or royal blue colors as symbols of Christ's Kingship and his restoration of the peaceable kingdom. Most prominent are the Advent candles that employ those colors. Some churches replace one purple candle with a pink one, representing the joy of the Virgin Mary as she prepared to give birth to the Christ child.

RED AND GREEN FOR CHRISTMAS Tradition has it that "paradise plays" of the fourteenth century introduced the Christmas tree and its decorations to us, harkening back to the Tree of Life, the fruit of the Tree of the Knowledge of Good and Evil, and the fall of man. From this medieval tradition, we recall these symbols in the colors green and red.

WHITE AND/OR GOLD FOR CHRISTMAS AND EPIPHANY The white and gold colors of these seasons symbolize the glory of God expressed in Christ dwelling among us. For instance, the Christ candle in the Advent wreath is usually white.

POMEGRANATE The pomegranate is a symbol used throughout the Scriptures and is associated with family blessing, life, and fullness. The Eastern Orthodox Church employs the pomegranate as a symbol of the heavenly kingdom, which will come to fruition in Christ, with the seeds of the kingdom placed here on earth. This symbol may be incorporated in the use of fruit or pomegranate flavored drinks.

CLOVES Similar to their use on the Paschal candle at Easter, cloves are often used as a substitute for incense and are associated with the frankincense given to Jesus. This symbol given by the Magi represented Christ's sacrifice, Christ's divinity, and his priestly role.

MINT Mint is often associated with healing. We use it to remind us of the prophecies concerning Jesus Christ as a healer. In two separate healing accounts in Matthew, the Scriptures refer to Isaiah's prophecies about Jesus' healing ministry (see Matthew 8:16–17 and Isaiah 53:4; Matthew 12:15–21 and Isaiah 42:1–4).

PEACHES AND PEARS Peaches and pears represent the Christ child as the fruit of salvation and are prominent in paintings of Jesus and Mary throughout church history.

ALMONDS Numbers 17 refers to the budding rod of Aaron as an almond blossom. From this reference the early church employed the almond as both a symbol of the Virgin Mary's purity and the virgin birth of Jesus.

LILY The lily has a rich symbolic history and has been most often used to reflect the purity and innocence of Mary and the virgin birth.

HOME GATHERING FOR WINTER

THE CELEBRATION OF THE KING The home gathering for this season focuses on the incarnation of Jesus and is driven largely by historic customs surrounding Epiphany. This home gathering is usually celebrated the weekend of or the one immediately following the day of Epiphany.

The Lighting of the Candle

LEADER   Jesus, Light of the Nations, fill our home with your peace.

A participant lights the candle for the season.[6]

MEMBER   We praise you, God, King of the Universe, for you have given us Jesus Christ, our Immanuel, God with us.

EVERYONE   We praise you, God, Creator and Redeemer.

LEADER   Father, by your Holy Spirit, you blessed your servant Mary with a son, our Lord Jesus Christ. Because of your presence, may our bodies and souls be renewed in the peace and rest of this day and in the joy of this season. *Amen.*

The Blessing

Families with children may want to insert a short prayer for each child here.

LEADER   May God guard our hearts, minds, and home in Christ Jesus.

Song of Blessing ✠

The Lord bless you and keep you;
The Lord make his face shine upon you.
The Lord be gracious to you.
And give you his peace, forever.

Telling the Redemptive Story

The questions below are designed for children. Older groups may omit them.

LEADER   What do we celebrate during the Advent season?

CHILDREN   God sent his Son, Jesus, born of the Virgin Mary, by the power of the Holy Spirit.

LEADER   How did we know Jesus was the Son of God?

CHILDREN   He fulfilled all the promises and prophecies of the old covenant, told over thousands of years.

LEADER   Why did Jesus come to earth?

CHILDREN   To reconcile us to God and restore us to the image of our Creator.

If the questions are omitted, the liturgy continues here.

LEADER   This Advent season, we anticipate the birth of the King, Jesus Christ, the Savior of the world and the fulfillment of all of God's promises.

We look forward to his return, when he will establish his peaceable kingdom forever.

Readings for the Season[7] ✚

The Advent wreath has four blue candles and one larger white candle.

FIRST WEEK OF ADVENT—THE PATRIARCHS

THE ADVENT WREATH *A participant lights the candle of the patriarchs and reads:*
A promise was given to the patriarchs: "I see him, but not now; I behold him, but not near: A star shall come out of Jacob, and a scepter shall rise out of Israel." Numbers 24:17
Additional Reading: Genesis 12:1–3; Genesis 49:9–10; Romans 9:5
Weekday liturgies for this week are found on page 41

SECOND WEEK OF ADVENT—THE PROPHETS

THE ADVENT WREATH *Light the candle of the prophets:*

Hundreds of years before the birth of Christ, Isaiah prophesied: "For to us a child is born, to us a son is given; and the government shall be upon his shoulder, and his name shall be called Wonderful, Counselor, Mighty God, Everlasting Father, Prince of Peace." Isaiah 9:6

Additional Reading: Micah 5:2; Isaiah 2:3–4; 1 Chronicles 17:9–15
Weekday liturgies for this week are found on page 43.

THIRD WEEK OF ADVENT—JOHN THE BAPTIST

THE ADVENT WREATH *Light the candle of John the Baptist:*
Of John the Baptist, it was foretold: "Behold, I send my messenger, and he will prepare the way before me. And the Lord whom you seek will suddenly come to his temple." Malachi 3:1
Additional Reading: Isaiah 40:3–5; John 1:6–9
Weekday liturgies for this week are found on page 45.

FOURTH WEEK OF ADVENT—MARY THE MOTHER OF GOD

THE ADVENT WREATH: *Light the candle of Mary the Mother of God:*
Mary said: "My soul magnifies the Lord, and my spirit rejoices in God my Savior." Luke 1:46–47
Additional Reading: Luke 1:46–55
Weekday liturgies for this week are found on page 47.

For the lighting of the Christ candle, see the liturgy for Christmas Day on page 71.

ADDITIONAL Over dinner, older groups may want to engage in creative, explorative discussion of the Scriptures, in the ancient tradition of Midrash.[8]

Blessing the Cup

LEADER We praise you, God, King of the Universe. You have given us the fruit of the vine. Father, you sent your son, Jesus, to shed his blood for our reconciliation and the redemption of the world.

The leader pours the wine or juice and passes the cup so everyone drinks.

Blessing the Bread and Oil

LEADER We praise you, God, King of the Universe. You have given us bread from the earth. Jesus, you told us, "I am the bread of life. Anyone who comes to me will never go hungry."

LEADER We also praise you, God, King of the Universe. You give us this oil. Holy Spirit, you have come to give us new life. Just as you led Jesus, our teacher, lead us. We not only remember Christ's death, but we also celebrate his birth, his iife, and the power of his resurrection.

EVERYONE We celebrate the birth, life, death, resurrection, ascension, and return of our King, Jesus Christ.

Everyone takes the bread, dips into the oil, and eats.

LEADER God, during this season of Advent, as we anticipate the coming of our Savior, dispel the darkness of sin and enlighten our hearts. May the symbols and stories of this season remind us of Christ's promise to bring salvation and restoration to the world.

Song of Celebration ✠

Sing a song of your choice.

The Peace of Sabbath

LEADER The peace of Christ be with you.

EVERYONE And also with you.

All pass the peace of Christ.

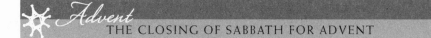
The Greeting

LEADER   The Lord be with you.

EVERYONE   And also with you.

LEADER   When we are together, the Christ in me sees the Christ in you. Wherever we go, whatever we do, the ground we walk together is holy ground.

The Lighting of the Two Candles

The questions below are designed for children. Older groups may omit them.

LEADER   We part from the Sabbath ceremoniously, just as we welcomed it. This evening, we tell the conclusion of God's redemptive plan and celebrate our hope in its completion.

LEADER   What do the two candles symbolize?

CHILDREN   The two natures of Jesus Christ: Jesus is completely God and completely man.

LEADER   Why is it important to understand that Jesus is both completely God and completely man?

CHILDREN   Jesus, the fullness of God, became man so that we could live a divine life.

LEADER   If Jesus were not completely God, his sacrifice would have been insufficient. If he were not completely man, there would be no hope for us to participate in his divine life.

If the questions are omitted, the liturgy continues here.

LEADER   During the season of Advent, the two candles remind us of the two natures of Christ—being completely God and completely human. Our Lord Jesus Christ is one and the same God, perfect in divinity and perfect in humanity, true God and true human.

God, you have expressed your unquenchable desire to redeem us and your creation. We praise you, God, King of the Universe, who created light. You have given us Jesus Christ, the fullness of God.

One of the participants lights the two candles.

The Cup of Blessing

The leader lifts the cup for all to see.

LEADER   We lift up the cup of salvation.

EVERYONE   For salvation belongs to our God.

LEADER   Father, your blessing be upon us, now and forever.

The leader places the cup in a dish.

LEADER   We praise you, God, King of the Universe. Pour out your blessing on us.

EVERYONE   Fill our cups to overflowing.

LEADER   May the blessing that you pour on us spill into the lives of those around us.

A participant places the cup in a dish and fills the cup until it overflows, then pours the remaining wine or juice into a cup for all other participants.

Short Prayer for the Week

LEADER   Though we know the truth of God's redemptive story, we often forget God. We become so accustomed to the world around us that we often blend in without thinking. These short prayers reconnect our spirits back to God's Spirit, asking him to tune our ears and refocus our attention to his work and our identity in Christ.

FIRST WEEK OF ADVENT—THE PATRIARCHS
Jesus, Joy of my heart, teach me the way of faith.

SECOND WEEK OF ADVENT—THE PROPHETS
Immanuel, hope of the nations, come and save me.

THIRD WEEK OF ADVENT—JOHN THE BAPTIST
Holy Spirit, keep me alert as I wait for the day of Christ's coming.

FOURTH WEEK OF ADVENT—MARY THE MOTHER OF JESUS
Spirit of Christ, grant me endurance as I wait for the coming kingdom.

Conclusion of the Day of Rest

LEADER   We now depart from our day of rest. Tomorrow we return to work. But we anticipate God's overflowing blessing on our lives this week. We long for our next day of rest as we long for the final day of rest, where we will enjoy a great banquet hosted by Jesus Christ our King.

MEMBER   God will prepare a feast with the best food and the greatest of aged wines.

LEADER   What do you think the great banquet will look like? What do you think we will eat? What will the music be like?

The participants imagine the great banquet.
A participant lights the incense and wafts it through the room.

LEADER   We praise you, God, King of the Universe, for you have given us our memories, our desires, and our senses. With great joy we remember the sweetness of this day of rest and anticipate the great day of rest to come.

Song for the Season ✠
Sing a song of your choice.

Blessing of the Week

LEADER   Jesus, during this Advent season, may we remember that though you are fully God, you chose to humble yourself, making yourself nothing, taking the nature of a servant, being made in human likeness. Like you, may we humble ourselves, living the truth of your gospel in our home and everywhere we go. *Amen.*

The Lighting of the Candle

LEADER   Jesus, Son of David, light our path with your salvation.

A participant lights the Christ candle from the Advent wreath.

MEMBER   We praise you, God, King of the Universe, for you have given us Jesus Christ, the King of nations, the Joy of our hearts.

EVERYONE   We praise you, God, Creator and Redeemer.

LEADER   Loving Father, this Christmas we remember the birth of Jesus, so that we may share in the song of the angels, the gladness of the shepherds, and worship of the Wise Men. Because you came to earth, we enjoy your presence. May our bodies and souls be renewed in the peace and rest of this day and the joy of this season.

The Blessing

Families with children may want to insert a short prayer for each child here.

LEADER   May this Christmas bring peace and joy to our home and the homes of those we love.

Song of Blessing ✠

The Lord bless you and keep you;
The Lord make his face shine upon you.
The Lord be gracious to you.
And give you his peace, forever.

Telling the Redemptive Story

The questions below are designed for children. Older groups may omit them.

LEADER   What do we celebrate during Christmas?

CHILDREN   Jesus was born so that we might live freely with God.

LEADER   In what way did Jesus come to earth?

CHILDREN   He was born in a humble stable, into a poor family.

LEADER   Why did Jesus come into a poor family?

CHILDREN   Though he was rich, he became poor so that through his poverty we might become rich.

If the questions are omitted, the liturgy continues here.

LEADER This Christmas, we celebrate the birth of the Eternal King, Jesus Christ. Through his life heaven and earth were reconciled. Our Great King shared in our weakness so that we might share in his glory. May the light of Jesus, the Incarnate Word, shine in our home now and forever. *Amen.*

Readings for the Season ✠

First Week of Christmas—The Nativity of Jesus

The angels announced the good news that would change past, present, and future: "Unto you is born this day in the city of David a Savior, who is Christ the Lord." Luke 2:11

Additional Reading: Luke 2:11–14
Weekday liturgies for this week are found on page 49

SECOND WEEK OF CHRISTMAS—ARRIVAL OF THE MAGI[9]

The men from the East recognized the Christ child as the True King: "And going into the house they saw the child with Mary his mother, and they fell down and worshiped him." Matthew 2:11

Additional Reading: Matthew 2:1–12
Weekday liturgies for this week are found on page 51

ADDITIONAL Over dinner, older groups may want to engage in creative, explorative discussion of the Scriptures, in the ancient tradition of Midrash.

Blessing the Cup

LEADER We praise you, God, King of the Universe, for you have given us the fruit of the vine. Father, you sent your son, the Incarnate Word, the flesh and blood of God.
The leader pours the wine or juice and passes the cup so everyone drinks.

Blessing the Bread and Oil

LEADER We praise you, God, King of the Universe, for you give us bread from the earth and you sent Jesus Christ to be born in Bethlehem,[10] the city of David.

LEADER We praise you, God, King of the Universe, for you give us this oil. Holy Spirit, you anointed Jesus to preach the good news to the poor.

EVERYONE We celebrate the birth, life, death, resurrection, ascension, and return of our King, Jesus Christ.
Everyone takes the bread, dips into the oil, and eats.

LEADER During this Christmas season, may God remind us of the peace given to us through Jesus Christ, the Prince of Peace. May the joy of this season radiate its brilliance in our lives and in our home.

Song of Celebration ⊕

The family or group may sing a song of its choice.

The Peace of Sabbath

LEADER The peace of Christ be with you.

EVERYONE And also with you.

All pass the peace of Christ.

Christmas
THE CLOSING OF SABBATH FOR CHRISTMAS

The Greeting

LEADER The Lord be with you.

EVERYONE And also with you.

LEADER When we are together, the Christ in me sees the Christ in you. Wherever we go, whatever we do, the ground we walk together is holy ground.

The Lighting of the Two Candles

The questions below are designed for children. Older groups may omit them.

LEADER We part from the Sabbath ceremoniously, just as we welcomed it. This evening, we tell the conclusion of God's redemptive plan and celebrate our hope in its completion.

LEADER What do the two candles symbolize?

CHILDREN The two natures of Jesus Christ: Jesus is completely God and completely man.

LEADER Why is it important to understand that Jesus is both completely God and completely man?

CHILDREN Jesus, the fullness of God, became man so that we could live a divine life.

LEADER If Jesus were not completely God, his sacrifice would have been insufficient. If he were not completely man, there would be no hope for us to participate in his divine life.

If the questions are omitted, the liturgy continues here.

LEADER   This Christmas, the two candles remind us of the two natures of Christ—being completely God and completely human. Our Lord Jesus Christ is one and the same God, perfect in divinity and perfect in humanity, true God and true human.

God, you have expressed your unquenchable desire to redeem us and your creation. We praise you, God, King of the Universe, who created light. You have given us Jesus Christ, the fullness of God.

The Cup of Blessing
The leader lifts the cup for all to see.

LEADER   We lift up the cup of salvation.

EVERYONE   For salvation belongs to our God.

LEADER   Father, your blessing be upon us now and forever.

The leader places the cup in a dish.

LEADER   We praise you, God, King of the Universe, for you have given us the fruit of the vine and you generously pour out your blessing on us.

EVERYONE   Fill our cups to overflowing.

LEADER   May the blessing that you pour on us spill over into the lives of those around us.

A participant places the cup in a dish and fills the cup until it overflows, then pours the remaining wine or juice into a cup for each member.

Short Prayer for the Week

LEADER   Though we know the truth of God's redemptive story, we often forget God. We become so accustomed to the world around us that we often blend in without thinking. These short prayers reconnect our spirits back to God's Spirit, asking him to tune our ears and refocus our attention to his work and our identity in Christ.

FIRST WEEK OF CHRISTMAS—THE NATIVITY OF JESUS
Jesus, Word of God, enable me to welcome your love.

SECOND WEEK OF CHRISTMAS—ARRIVAL OF THE MAGI[11]
Just as you did with the Wise Men, place in me a heart of true worship.

Conclusion of the Day of Rest

LEADER   We now depart from our day of rest. Tomorrow we return to work, even as we anticipate God's overflowing blessing on our lives this week. In returning to our work, we also long for our next day of rest as we long for the final day of rest, where we will enjoy a great banquet hosted by Jesus Christ our King.

MEMBER   God will prepare a feast with the best food and the greatest of aged wines.

LEADER   What do you think the great banquet will look like? What do you think we will eat? What will the music be like?

The participants imagine the great banquet.
A participant lights the incense and wafts it through the room.

LEADER   We praise you, God, King of the Universe, for you have given us our memories, our desires, and our senses. With great joy we remember the sweetness of this day of rest and anticipate the day of rest to come.

Song for the Season ✚

Sing a song of your choice.

Blessing of the Week

LEADER   This Christmas season may we remember that even though you came as a small child, you brought us the greatest of all gifts—the gift of eternal love. May your love penetrate the inner depths of our hearts and every corner of this home. *Amen.*

The Lighting of the Candle

LEADER Lord Jesus, may your light illumine our souls. Lead us by your presence that we may love and worship you in all things.

This liturgy may continue to use the Christ candle from the previous season.

MEMBER We praise you, God, King of the Universe, for you have given us Jesus Christ, the Incarnate Word.

EVERYONE We praise you, God, our Creator and Redeemer.

LEADER All-powerful Father, Christ your Son became man for us. He followed the leading of your Spirit to empower us with a divine life. May he free our hearts from sin and bring us into your presence, and may that presence renew our bodies and souls in the peace and rest of this day.

The Blessing

Families with children may want to insert a short prayer for each child here.

LEADER May Jesus Christ, the Word of God, bless us and allow all of us in this home to live in peace and blessing.

Song of Blessing ✦

The Lord bless you and keep you;
The Lord make his face shine upon you.
The Lord be gracious to you.
And give you his peace, forever.

Telling the Redemptive Story

The questions below are designed for children. Older groups may omit them.

LEADER What do we celebrate during this season?

CHILDREN That Jesus Christ, the Word of God, lived among us.

LEADER Why was Jesus baptized?

CHILDREN To demonstrate his submission to the Father by the leading of the Spirit.

LEADER Why did Jesus become human?

CHILDREN He became human that we might become divine.

If the questions are omitted, the liturgy continues here.

LEADER   During this season, we celebrate the life of our teacher, Jesus Christ. The entirety of Christ's life was a continual teaching: his words, his healings, his miracles, his prayers, his love for people, his special affection for the poor, his acceptance of his sacrifice on the cross for the redemption of the world, and his resurrection are the fulfillment of all truth.

Readings for the Season ✠

WINTER HOME GATHERING—THE CELEBRATION OF THE KING
See the liturgy for this home gathering on page 72.
Weekday liturgies for this week are found on page 53.

EPIPHANY—SECOND WEEK AFTER CHRISTMAS
The first words of Jesus' ministry announce, "The time is fulfilled, and the kingdom of God is at hand; repent and believe in the gospel." Mark 1:15
Additional Reading: Mark 1:9–16
Weekday liturgies for this week are found on page 55.

EPIPHANY—THIRD WEEK AFTER CHRISTMAS
Jesus revealed the essence of the Law: "Do not think that I have come to abolish the Law or the Prophets; I have not come to abolish them but to fulfill them." Matthew 5:17
Additional Reading: Matthew 5:1–17
Weekday liturgies for this week are found on page 57.

EPIPHANY—FOURTH WEEK AFTER CHRISTMAS
Jesus called Simon Peter, James, and John to follow him: "They left everything and followed him." Luke 5:11
Additional Reading: Luke 5:1–11
Weekday liturgies for this week are found on page 59.

ADDITIONAL   Over dinner, older groups may want to engage in creative, explorative discussion of the Scriptures, in the ancient tradition of Midrash. See Appendix E.

Blessing the Cup

LEADER   We praise you, God, King of the Universe, for you have given us the fruit of the vine. Jesus, in your first miracle you turned water into wine, making common things divine.

The leader pours the wine or juice and passes the cup so everyone drinks.

Blessing the Bread and Oil

LEADER   We praise you, God, King of the Universe, for you give us bread from the earth. Jesus, when you fed the crowds, you blessed the bread, replacing need with abundance.

LEADER   We also praise you, God, King of the Universe, for you give us this oil. Spirit, sent by the Father, you led Jesus throughout his life—into the wilderness, empowering the miraculous, healing the suffering, leading the lost, teaching the confused, revealing his divinity, sustaining him through his trials, and resurrecting him from death to life.

EVERYONE   We celebrate the birth, life, death, resurrection, ascension, and return of our King, Jesus Christ.

Everyone takes the bread, dips into the oil, and eats.

LEADER   As followers of Jesus, may God bless us as we continue to walk to his Spirit and submit to his leadership. May our faith, the root of the divine life, produce fruit that can only come from a life submitted to God.

Song of Celebration
Sing a song of your choice.

The Peace of Sabbath

LEADER   The peace of Christ be with you.

EVERYONE   And also with you.

All pass the peace of Christ.

THE CLOSING OF SABBATH FOR EPIPHANY

The Greeting

LEADER   The Lord be with you.

EVERYONE   And also with you.

LEADER   When we are together, the Christ in me sees the Christ in you. Wherever we go, whatever we do, the ground we walk together is holy ground.

The Lighting of the Two Candles

The questions below are designed for children. Older groups may omit them.

LEADER   We part from the Sabbath ceremoniously, just as we welcomed it. This evening, we tell the conclusion of God's redemptive plan and celebrate our hope in its completion.

LEADER What do the two candles symbolize?

CHILDREN The two natures of Jesus Christ: Jesus is completely God and completely man.

LEADER Why is it important to understand that Jesus is both completely God and completely man?

CHILDREN Jesus, the fullness of God, became man so that we could live a divine life.

LEADER If Jesus were not completely God, his sacrifice would have been insufficient. If he were not completely man, there would be no hope for us to participate in his divine life.

If the questions are omitted, the liturgy continues here.

LEADER During the season of Epiphany, the two candles remind us of the two natures of Christ—being completely God and completely human. The one who spoke Creation into existence humbled himself to live as one of us. In doing so, he gave us the gift of living a divine life in the power of his Spirit.

LEADER We praise you God, King of the Universe, who created light. Father, you have given us freedom to live a divine life in your Spirit.

One of the participants lights the two candles.

Song for the Season ☦

Sing a song of your choice.

The Cup of Blessing

The leader lifts the cup for all to see.

LEADER We lift up the cup of salvation.

EVERYONE For salvation belongs to our God.

LEADER Father, your blessing be upon us now and forever.

The leader places the cup in a dish.

LEADER We praise you, God, King of the Universe, for you have given us the fruit of the vine and you generously pour out your blessing on us.

EVERYONE Fill our cups to overflowing.

LEADER May the blessing that you pour on us spill over into the lives of those around us.

A participant places the cup in a dish and fills the cup until it overflows, then pours the remaining wine or juice into a cup for each member.

Short Prayer for the Week

LEADER Though we know the truth of God's redemptive story, we often forget God. We become so accustomed to the world around us that we often blend in without thinking. These short prayers reconnect our spirits back to God's Spirit, asking him to tune our ears and refocus our attention to his work and our identity in Christ.

EPIPHANY—FIRST WEEK AFTER CHRISTMAS
Beloved Son, fill me with the peace of your Holy Spirit.

EPIPHANY—SECOND WEEK AFTER CHRISTMAS
Jesus, grant us the wisdom to seek your kingdom.

EPIPHANY—THIRD WEEK AFTER CHRISTMAS
Teacher, instruct me in the law of your love.

EPIPHANY—FOURTH WEEK AFTER CHRISTMAS
Lord, give me the faith to leave my own desires and follow you.

Conclusion of the Day of Rest

LEADER We now depart from our day of rest. Tomorrow we return to work even as we anticipate God's overflowing blessing on our lives this week. In returning to our work, we also long for our next day of rest as we long for the final day of rest, where we will enjoy a great banquet hosted by Jesus Christ our King.

MEMBER God will prepare a feast with the best food and the greatest of aged wines.

LEADER What do you think the great banquet will look like? What do you think we will eat? What will the music be like?
The participants imagine the great banquet.
A participant lights the incense and wafts it through the room.

LEADER We praise you God, King of the Universe, for you have given us our memories, our desires, and our senses. With great joy we remember the sweetness of this day of rest and anticipate the day of rest to come.

Blessing of the Week

LEADER This season we celebrate your presentation at the temple, your baptism, your miracle at Cana, your announcement of the coming kingdom, and your invitation to become your disciples. You made it clear that God was living among us, making common things divine. Enlighten this home with the brilliance of your presence, that we may discover the truth of your redemption every day in our work and play. *Amen.*

The Lighting of the Candle ✠

LEADER   Jesus said, "I am the light of the world. Whoever follows me will not walk in darkness, but will have the light of life."

A participant lights the candle for the season.[13]

MEMBER   We praise you, God, King of the Universe, for you have given us Jesus Christ, our Savior, the Light of the World.

EVERYONE   We praise you, God, our Creator and Redeemer.

LEADER   We praise you, God, King of the Universe, for you have given us this day of rest. Bless our family and friends and lift us from every care and anxiety. May the light of this day burn brightly in our hearts and may it cast the radiance of its peace in our home and throughout the world. *Amen.*

The Blessing

Families with children may want to insert a short prayer for each child here.

LEADER   Come, Holy Spirit, fill this home with peace; renew us in the fire of your love.

Song of Blessing ✠

The Lord bless you and keep you;
The Lord make his face shine upon you.
The Lord be gracious to you.
And give you his peace, forever.

Telling the Redemptive Story

The questions below are designed for children. Older groups may omit them.

LEADER   What is the first thing we celebrate on Sabbath?

CHILDREN   God created the world.

LEADER   How does the redemptive story begin?

CHILDREN   "In the beginning God created the heavens and the earth."

LEADER   What does this tell us about reality and life?

CHILDREN   Reality is rooted in God's story. He welcomes us to live in the world he created.

If the questions are omitted, the liturgy continues here.

LEADER In remembering God's creation and anticipating its restoration, the redemptive story shapes the way we see ourselves, each other, and the world around us.

Readings for the Season ✚

FIRST WEEK OF WINTER ORDINARY TIME[14]

Though Jesus was God, he came as a humble servant: "Your attitude should be the same as that of Christ Jesus: Who, being in very nature God, did not consider equality with God something to be grasped, but made himself nothing, taking the very nature of a servant." Philippians 2:5–7 (NIV)

Additional Reading: Philippians 2:5–11
Weekday liturgies for this week are found on page 61.

SECOND WEEK OF WINTER ORDINARY TIME

God's grace alone has saved us: "But because of his great love for us, God, who is rich in mercy, made us alive with Christ even when we were dead in transgressions—it is by grace you have been saved." Ephesians 2:4–5 (NIV)

Additional Reading: Ephesians 2:4–10
Weekday liturgies for this week are found on page 63.

THIRD WEEK OF WINTER ORDINARY TIME[15]

Faith is the foundation of our life in God: "Now faith is the assurance of things hoped for, the conviction of things not seen. . . . And without faith it is impossible to please [God]." Hebrews 11:1, 6

Additional Reading: Hebrews 11:1–3
Weekday liturgies for this week are found on page 65.

FOURTH WEEK OF WINTER ORDINARY TIME

Though life may sometimes become difficult, our hope does not disappoint: "Hope does not disappoint us, because God has poured out his love into our hearts by the Holy Spirit, whom he has given us." Romans 5:5 (NIV)

Additional Reading: Romans 5:1–5
Weekday liturgies for this week are found on page 67.

FIFTH WEEK OF WINTER ORDINARY TIME

After all events are recorded and God's plan is complete only love remains forever: "Three things remain: faith, hope and love. But the greatest of these is love." 1 Corinthians 13:13 (NIV)

Additional Reading: 1 Corinthians 13:4–13
Weekday liturgies for this week are found on page 69.

ADDITIONAL Over dinner, older groups may want to engage in creative, explorative discussion of the Scriptures, in the ancient tradition of Midrash. See Appendix E.

Blessing the Cup

LEADER We praise you, God, King of the Universe, for you give us the fruit of the vine, you who have poured out your blood for your people.
The leader pours the wine or juice and passes the cup so everyone drinks.

Blessing the Bread and Oil

LEADER We praise you, God, King of the Universe, for you give us bread from the earth and you have given us the bread of life in Jesus Christ.

LEADER We also praise you, God, King of the Universe, for you give us this oil and you give us the newness of life in the Holy Spirit.

EVERYONE We celebrate the birth, life, death, resurrection, ascension, and return of our King, Jesus Christ.
Everyone takes the bread, dips into the oil, and eats.

LEADER May God bless our family with the peace of his kingdom. And may we, like a tree, be rooted deeply in him and in his ways. May our family enjoy the beauty of God's redemptive story, now and forever.

Song of Celebration ✠
Sing a song of your choice.

The Peace of Sabbath

LEADER The peace of Christ be with you.
EVERYONE And also with you.
All pass the peace of Christ.

The Greeting

LEADER   The Lord be with you.

EVERYONE   And also with you.

LEADER   When we are together, the Christ in me sees the Christ in you. Wherever we go, whatever we do, the ground we walk together is holy ground.

The Lighting of the Two Candles

The questions below are designed for children. Older groups may omit them.

LEADER   We part from the Sabbath ceremoniously, just as we welcomed it. This evening, we tell the conclusion of God's redemptive plan and celebrate our hope in its completion.

LEADER   What do the two candles symbolize?

CHILDREN   God has separated the holy from the common things.

LEADER   What has God set apart?

CHILDREN   God has set apart his people.

If the questions are omitted, the liturgy continues here.

LEADER   Just as God has set apart the Sabbath in order to bless the working week, God has also set apart his people. He has called out his people, the church, to bless, redeem, and restore the fallen world.

LEADER   We praise you, God, King of the Universe, who created light and set apart your people to be a kingdom of peacemakers.

One of the participants lights the two candles.

Song for the Season ✠

Sing a song of your choice.

The Cup of Blessing

The leader lifts the cup for all to see.

LEADER   We lift up the cup of salvation.

EVERYONE   For salvation belongs to our God.

LEADER   Father, your blessing be upon us now and forever.

The leader places the cup in a dish.

LEADER   We praise you, God, King of the Universe, for you have given us the fruit of the vine and you generously pour out your blessing on us.

EVERYONE   Fill our cups to overflowing.

LEADER   May the blessing that you pour on us spill over into the lives of those around us.

A participant places the cup in a dish and fills the cup until it overflows, then pours the remaining wine or juice into a cup for each member.

Short Prayer for the Week

LEADER   Though we know the truth of God's redemptive story, we often forget God. We become so accustomed to the world around us that we often blend in without thinking. These short prayers reconnect our spirits back to God's Spirit, asking him to tune our ears and refocus our attention to his work and our identity in Christ.

FIRST WEEK OF WINTER ORDINARY TIME[16]
Son of God, give to me a humble heart ready to serve.

SECOND WEEK OF WINTER ORDINARY TIME
Savior, let me extend grace as you have given grace to me.

THIRD WEEK OF WINTER ORDINARY TIME[17]
Father, increase my faith that I may gain understanding.

FOURTH WEEK OF WINTER ORDINARY TIME
Lord Jesus Christ, let me never be put to shame.

FIFTH WEEK OF WINTER ORDINARY TIME
Jesus, my Savior, teach me to love as you love.

Conclusion of the Day of Rest

LEADER   We now depart from our day of rest. Tomorrow we return to work even as we anticipate God's overflowing blessing on our lives this week. In returning to our work, we also long for our next day of rest as we long for the final day of rest where we will enjoy a great banquet hosted by Jesus Christ our King.

MEMBER   God will prepare a feast with the best food and the greatest of aged wines.

LEADER   What do you think the great banquet will look like? What do you think we will eat? What will the music be like?
The participants imagine the great banquet.
A participant lights the incense and wafts it through the room.

LEADER   We praise you, God, King of the Universe, for you have given us our memories, our desires, and our senses. With great joy we remember the sweetness of this day of rest and anticipate the day of rest to come.

Blessing of the Week

LEADER   May the grace of Christ our Savior, the love of God our Father, and the fellowship of the Spirit be with us throughout this week and forevermore. *Amen.*

The Patriarchs

The Lighting of the Candle

The leader prays as a participant lights the candle.[18]

LEADER   Let us pray. Jesus, Light of the Nations, fill our home with your peace.

Meditation or Silence ✠

After a moment of silence or a physical expression of prayer, the leader continues.[19]

LEADER   God, all of our hope is in you.

Psalm

MONDAY • Psalm 19:1–6   **TUESDAY** • Psalm 25:1–5   **WEDNESDAY** • Psalm 85:8–13
THURSDAY • Psalm 31:14–16   **FRIDAY** • Psalm 118:19–24

Song for the Season ✠

Sing a song of your choice.

Short Verse

READER   Christ comes from the Patriarchs. Paul wrote: "To them belong the patriarchs, and from [them] according to the flesh, is the Christ who is God over all." Romans 9:5

Short Prayer

READER   God, teach me to walk the way of faith as did our father Abraham.

Scripture Reading ✠

EVERYONE   Father, open our eyes that we might see the wonders of your truth.

MONDAY

The great story begins with God: "In the beginning, God created the heavens and the earth." Genesis 1:1

Additional Reading: Genesis 1:1–5; John 1:1–5

TUESDAY

We rebelled against God and rejected the perfection of his creation. To redeem the Fall, God made a promise. He told the serpent that One would come to defeat him: "He shall bruise your head, and you shall bruise his heel." Genesis 3:15

Additional Reading: Genesis 3:1–15; Romans 3:23–26

WEDNESDAY

A promise was given to Abraham: "I will make of you a great nation, and I will bless you and make your name great, so that you will be a blessing." Genesis 12:2

Additional Reading: Genesis 12:1–3; Hebrews 11:17–22; Romans 4:13–25

THURSDAY

The apostle Paul writes: "For I tell you that Christ has become a servant of the Jews on behalf of God's truth, to confirm the promises made to the patriarchs." Romans 15:8 (NIV)

Additional Reading: Romans 15:7–13

FRIDAY

An oracle was given: "I see him, but not now; I behold him, but not near: a star shall come out of Jacob, and a scepter shall rise out of Israel." Numbers 24:17

Additional Reading: Genesis 49:9–10; Numbers 24:15–19; Revelation 2:27–29

Open Intercession or Daily Intercession
For daily intercessions see Appendix F.

Prayer for the Week

God of the ancient and the anticipated, God of our ancestors, to you be praise and glory forever. You called our grandfathers to live by the light of faith and to journey in the hope of your promises.

God of Abraham, Isaac, and Jacob, and all the patriarchs of old, you are our Father too; your love is revealed to us in Jesus Christ, Son of God and the Son of David. Amen. —*Based on a prayer of the Church of England*

Song for the Season ✠
Sing a song of your choice.

Closing Prayer for the Advent Season

All-powerful God, with great hope we look forward to the coming of our Savior. Renew us as we wait for you. Even though language is insufficient to communicate our longing for you, let our hearts and lives express and reflect the hope and trust we have in you. Amen. —*Based on a prayer of the Church of England*

The Prophets

The Lighting of the Candle

The leader prays as a participant lights the candle.

LEADER   Let us pray. Jesus, Light of the Nations, fill our home with your peace.

Meditation or Silence ✚

After a moment of silence or a physical expression of prayer, the leader continues.

LEADER   God, our souls long after you.

Psalm

MONDAY • Psalm 72:1–14   **TUESDAY** • Psalm 98:1–4   **WEDNESDAY** • Psalm 122:1–9
THURSDAY • Psalm 24:1–6   **FRIDAY** • Psalm 79:8–9

Song for the Season ✚

Sing a song of your choice.

Short Verse

READER   The prophet Isaiah wrote: "For to us a child is born, to us a son is given; and the government shall be upon his shoulder, and his name shall be called Wonderful, Counselor, Mighty God, Everlasting Father, Prince of Peace." Isaiah 9:6

Short Prayer

READER   Jesus, hope of the nations, come and save me.

Scripture Reading

EVERYONE   Father, open our eyes that we might see the wonders of your truth.

MONDAY

The prophets all looked forward to the arrival of Jesus: "The gospel he promised beforehand through his prophets in the Holy Scriptures regarding his Son, who as to his human nature was a descendant of David, and who through the Spirit of holiness was declared with power to be the Son of God by his resurrection from the dead: Jesus Christ our Lord." Romans 1:2–4 (NIV)

Additional Reading: Romans 1:1–6

TUESDAY

For thousands of years, the prophets anticipated Jesus: "Blessed be the Lord God of Israel, for he has visited and redeemed his people and has raised up a horn of salvation for us in the house of his servant David, as he spoke by the mouth of his holy prophets from of old, that we should be saved from our enemies." Luke 1:68–71

Additional Reading: Luke 1:67–79

WEDNESDAY

Christ is greater than the greatest prophet, Moses: "Moses was faithful in all God's house as a servant, to testify to the things that were to be spoken later, but Christ is faithful over God's house as a son." Hebrews 3:5–6

Additional Reading: Exodus 2:1–10; Hebrews 3:1–6

THURSDAY

The prophets spoke, but Jesus came in flesh and blood: "But what God foretold by the mouth of all the prophets, that his Christ would suffer, he thus fulfilled." Acts 3:18

Additional Reading: Acts 3:11–26

FRIDAY

Jesus is the final word: "Long ago, at many times and in many ways, God spoke to our fathers by the prophets, but in these last days he has spoken to us by his Son, whom he appointed the heir of all things, through whom also he created the world." Hebrews 1:1–2

Additional Reading: Hebrews 1:1–6

Open Intercession or Daily Intercession

For daily intercessions see Appendix F.

Prayer for the Week

God our Father, you spoke through the prophets and told of a Savior who would bring peace. You helped them to spread the message of his coming kingdom. Help us, as we prepare to celebrate his birth, to share with those around us the good news of your power and love. Give us peace in our hearts and homes this season and show all the world God's love. Amen. —*Based on a prayer of the Church of England*

Song for the Season ✙

Sing a song of your choice.

Closing Prayer for the Advent Season

All-powerful God, with great hope we look forward to the coming of our Savior. Renew us as we wait for you. Even though language is insufficient to communicate our longing for you, let our hearts and lives express and reflect the hope and trust we have in you. Amen. —*Based on a prayer of the Church of England*

 THIRD WEEK OF ADVENT

John the Baptist

The Lighting of the Candle

The leader prays as a participant lights the candle.

LEADER   Let us pray. Jesus, Light of the Nations, fill our home with your peace.

Meditation or Silence ✚

After a moment of silence or a physical expression of prayer, the leader continues.

LEADER   God, we come to you with a simple faith.

Psalm

MONDAY • Psalm 2:1–12   TUESDAY • Psalm 33:1–8   WEDNESDAY • Psalm 89:26–37
THURSDAY • Psalm 18:1–19   FRIDAY • Psalm 68:1–10

Song for the Season ✚

Sing a song of your choice.

Short Verse

READER   The apostle John wrote of Jesus: "All things were made through him, and without him was not any thing made that was made. In him was life, and the life was the light of men." John 1:3–4

Short Prayer

READER   Holy Spirit, keep me alert as I wait for the day of Christ's coming.

Scripture Reading

EVERYONE   Father, open our eyes that we might see the wonders of your truth.

MONDAY

Zechariah prophesied over his son John and told of the coming Messiah: "Blessed be the Lord God of Israel, for he has visited and redeemed his people and has raised up a horn of salvation for us in the house of his servant David, as he spoke by the mouth of his holy prophets from of old, that we should be saved from our enemies." Luke 1:68–71

Additional Reading: Luke 1:67–79

TUESDAY

The Scriptures foretold of one who would come before the Messiah: "See, I will send my messenger, who will prepare the way before me." Malachi 3:1 (NIV)

Additional Reading: Isaiah 40:1–5

WEDNESDAY

John, the second Elijah, came: "To bear witness about the light, that all might believe through him." John 1:7

Additional Reading: John 1:6–8; 1 Kings 18:20–40

THURSDAY

Just as the prophet said, John was the voice in the wilderness crying out: "Make straight the way of the Lord." John 1:23

Additional Reading: John 1:19–35

FRIDAY

Gabriel told Zechariah of his soon-arriving son, John: "He will be filled with the Holy Spirit, even from his mother's womb. And he will turn many of the children of Israel to the Lord their God . . . to make ready for the Lord a people prepared." Luke 1:15–17

Additional Reading: Luke 1:8–25

Open Intercession or Daily Intercession
For daily intercessions see Appendix F.

Prayer for the Week
Jesus, our Savior and King of the Ages, John told the people to prepare, for you were very near. As Christmas grows closer day by day, help us to be ready to welcome you in our homes. *Amen. —Based on a prayer of the Church of England*

Song for the Season

Sing a song of your choice.

Closing Prayer for the Advent Season

All-powerful God, with great hope we look forward to the coming of our Savior. Renew us as we wait for you. Even though language is insufficient to communicate our longing for you, let our hearts and lives express and reflect the hope and trust we have in you. Amen. *—Based on a prayer of the Church of England*

 FOURTH WEEK OF ADVENT

Mary the Mother of Jesus

The Lighting of the Candle

The leader prays as a participant lights the candle.

LEADER Let us pray. Jesus, Light of the Nations, fill our home with your peace.

Meditation or Silence

After a moment of silence or a physical expression of prayer, the leader continues.

LEADER In your presence, our spirits rejoice.

Song for the Season

Sing a song of your choice.

Psalm

MONDAY • Psalm 110:1–7   **TUESDAY** • Psalm 85:1–7   **WEDNESDAY** • Psalm 45:3–5
THURSDAY • Psalm 132:1–5, 11–18   **FRIDAY** • Psalm 40:4–8

Short Verse

READER Mary prayed: "My soul magnifies the Lord, and my spirit rejoices in God my Savior." Luke 1:46–47

Short Prayer

READER Spirit of Christ, give me endurance as I wait for the coming kingdom.

Scripture Reading

EVERYONE   Father, open our eyes that we might see the wonders of your truth.

MONDAY

Mary rejoiced in God's faithfulness: "He has helped his servant Israel, in remembrance of his mercy, as he spoke to our fathers, to Abraham and to his offspring forever." Luke 1:54–55

Additional Reading: Genesis 17:19; Luke 1:46–56

TUESDAY

Isaiah said to the house of David: "The LORD himself will give you a sign: The virgin will be with child and will give birth to a son, and will call him Immanuel." Isaiah 7:14 (NIV)

Additional Reading: Isaiah 7:13–15; Matthew 1:18–25

WEDNESDAY

Jesus fulfilled Isaiah's prophecy: "The Spirit of the Sovereign LORD is on me, because he has anointed me to proclaim good news to the poor." Isaiah 61:1

Additional Reading: Isaiah 61:1–4; Luke 4:16–21

THURSDAY

Jeremiah prophesied and God fulfilled it in Jesus: "I will raise up for David a righteous Branch, and he shall reign as king and deal wisely." Jeremiah 23:5

Additional Reading: Jeremiah 23:1–6; Ezekiel 34:23–24; John 10:7–18

FRIDAY

Through the prophet Amos God promised: "In that day I will restore the fallen house of David." Amos 9:11–12 (NLT)

Additional Reading: Amos 9:11–15; Acts 15:12–18

Open Intercession or Daily Intercession

For daily intercessions see Appendix F.

Prayer for the Week

Father, your light has shone in our darkened world through the child-bearing of the blessed Mary; grant that we who have seen your glory may daily be renewed in your image and prepared like Mary for the coming of your Son, who is the Lord and Savior of all. *Amen. —Based on a prayer of the Church of England*

Song for the Season ✠

Sing a song of your choice.

Closing Prayer for the Advent Season

All-powerful God, with great hope we look forward to the coming of our Savior. Renew us as we wait for you. Even though language is insufficient to communicate our longing for you, let our hearts and lives express and reflect the hope and trust we have in you. Amen. —*Based on a prayer of the Church of England*

Christmas

FIRST WEEK OF CHRISTMAS

The Nativity of Jesus

The Lighting of the Candle

The leader prays as a participant lights the Christ candle.

LEADER Let us pray. Father, with the birth of Jesus, your glory breaks into the world.

Meditation or Silence

After a moment of silence or a physical expression of prayer, the leader continues.

LEADER Father, in your presence we are complete.

Psalm

MONDAY • Psalm 145:1–9 **TUESDAY** • Psalm 146:1–10

WEDNESDAY • Psalm 147:1–6

THURSDAY • Psalm 148:1–6 **FRIDAY** • Psalm 149:1–4

Song for the Season

Sing a song of your choice.

Short Verse

READER The angels said: "Glory to God in the highest, and on earth peace to those with whom he is pleased." Luke 2:14

Short Prayer

READER Jesus, Word of God, enable me to welcome your love.

Scripture Reading

EVERYONE   Father, open our eyes that we might see the wonders of your Truth.

MONDAY

Angels came to announce the birth of the King: "Glory to God in the highest, and on earth peace to those with whom he is pleased." Luke 2:14

Additional Reading: Luke 2:1–14

TUESDAY

Jesus fully revealed God to us: "In the beginning was the Word, and the Word was with God, and the Word was God." John 1:1

Additional Reading: John 1:1–18

WEDNESDAY

The apostle Paul told us: "According to [God's] purpose, which he set forth in Christ as a plan for the fullness of time, to unite all things in him, things in heaven and things on earth." Ephesians 1:10

Additional Reading: Ephesians 1:3–14

THURSDAY

Jesus is the fulfillment of the universe: "He is before all things, and in him all things hold together." Colossians 1:17

Additional Reading: Colossians 1:15–20

FRIDAY

The humble child will return as a conquering King: "Then I saw heaven opened, and behold, a white horse! The one sitting on it is called Faithful and True. . . . On his robe and on his thigh he has a name written, King of kings and Lord of lords." Revelation 19:11, 16

Additional Reading: Revelation 19:6–16

Open Intercession or Daily Intercession
For daily intercessions see Appendix F.

Prayer for the Week

Blessed are you, Sovereign Lord, King of Peace: To you be praise and glory forever. The new light of Jesus, your Incarnate Word, gives gladness in our sorrow, and a presence in our isolation. Fill our lives with your light, until they overflow with gladness and praise. Blessed be you, God, forever. *Amen. —Based on a prayer of the Church of England*

Song for the Season
Sing a song of your choice.

Closing Prayer for Christmas

Lord, now you let your servant depart in peace according to your word. For my eyes have seen your salvation, which you have prepared before the face of all people, a light to enlighten the Gentiles and the glory of your people Israel. Glory to God the Father, the Son, and the Holy Spirit. As it was in the beginning, is now and so shall be forever, world without end. *Amen. —Based on the Nunc Dimittis, Luke 2:29–32*

 SECOND WEEK OF CHRISTMAS

Arrival of the Magi

Note: Depending on the liturgical dates for this year, this week's liturgy may or may not be necessary. See the table in Appendix B or the athomewithgod.org website for exact dates for this year.

The Lighting of the Candle
The leader prays as a participant lights the Christ candle.

LEADER   Let us pray. Father, with the birth of Jesus, your glory breaks into the world.

Meditation or Silence
After a moment of silence or a physical expression of prayer, the leader continues.

LEADER   Father, in your presence we are complete.

Psalm
MONDAY • Psalm 98:1–3   **TUESDAY** • Psalm 138:1–8   **WEDNESDAY** • Psalm 67:1–7
THURSDAY • Psalm 72:5–11   **FRIDAY** • Psalm 24:1–10

Song for the Season
Sing a song of your choice.

Short Verse
READER   Simeon spoke for the expectant people of God when he said: "My eyes have seen your salvation that you have prepared in the presence of all peoples, a light for revelation to the Gentiles and for glory to your people Israel." Luke 2:30–32

Short Prayer

READER   Just as you did with the Wise Men, place in me a heart of true worship.

Scripture Reading

EVERYONE   Father, open our eyes that we might see the wonders of your truth.

MONDAY

Jesus fulfilled the prophecy of Hosea: "Out of Egypt I called my son." Matthew 2:15
Additional Reading: Matthew 2:13–18

TUESDAY

The Wise Men from the East followed the star: "On coming to the house, they saw the child with his mother Mary, and they bowed down and worshiped him." Matthew 2:11
Additional Reading: Matthew 2:1–16

WEDNESDAY

Jesus grew and gained wisdom: "And the child grew and became strong, filled with wisdom. And the favor of God was upon him." Luke 2:40
Additional Reading: Luke 2:36–40

THURSDAY

The first words of Jesus' ministry were: "The kingdom of God is near. Repent and believe the good news!" Mark 1:15 (NIV)
Additional Reading: Mark 1:1–15

FRIDAY

Jesus told the woman at the well: "The water that I will give him will become in him a spring of water welling up to eternal life." John 4:14
Additional Reading: John 4:1–25

Open Intercession or Daily Intercession
For daily intercessions see Appendix F.

Prayer for the Week

Loving Father, help us remember the birth of Jesus that we may share in the song of the angels, the gladness of the shepherds, and the worship of the Wise Men. Close the door of hate and open the door of love all over the world. *Amen.* —*Based on a prayer by Robert Louis Stevenson*

Song for the Season
Sing a song of your choice.

Closing Prayer for Christmas

Lord, now you let your servant depart in peace according to your word. For my eyes have seen your salvation, which you have prepared before the face of all people, a light to enlighten the Gentiles and the glory of your people Israel. Glory to God the Father, the Son and to the Holy Spirit. As it was in the beginning, is now and so shall be forever, world without end. *Amen. —Based on the Nunc Dimittis, Luke 2:29–32*

Epiphany FIRST WEEK AFTER CHRISTMAS

The Lighting of the Candle
The leader prays as a participant lights the Christ candle.

LEADER   Let us pray, "Lord Jesus, may your light shine our way. Lead us by your presence that we may love and worship you in all things."

Meditation or Silence

After a moment of silence or a physical expression of prayer, the leader continues.

LEADER   Spirit, renew us with a childlike faith.

Psalm

MONDAY • Psalm 130:1–8   **TUESDAY** • Psalm 3:1–8   **WEDNESDAY** • Psalm 31:1–5
THURSDAY • Psalm 19:7–11   **FRIDAY** • Psalm 23:1–6

Song for the Season
Sing a song of your choice.

Short Verse

READER   Jesus said: "Seek first the kingdom of God and his righteousness, and all these things will be added to you." Matthew 6:33

Short Prayer

READER   Beloved Son, fill me with the peace of your Holy Spirit.

Scripture Reading

EVERYONE   Father, open our eyes that we might see the wonders of your truth.

MONDAY

John prepared the way for one who would baptize with the Holy Spirit and with fire: "I baptize you with water for repentance, but he who is coming after me is mightier than I, whose sandals I am not worthy to carry. He will baptize you with the Holy Spirit and fire." Matthew 3:11

Additional Reading: Matthew 3:1–12

TUESDAY

At Jesus' baptism the Spirit descended and the Father spoke to Jesus: "You are my Son, whom I love; with you I am well pleased." Luke 3:22 (NIV)

Additional Reading: Luke 3:15–22

WEDNESDAY

The Spirit led Jesus to the wilderness where he lived on the bread of the words of his Father: And Jesus answered him, "It is written, 'Man shall not live by bread alone.'" Luke 4:4

Additional Reading: Luke 4:1–13

THURSDAY

Jesus gave us the first of his miraculous signs, turning water into wine: "This, the first of his signs, Jesus did at Cana in Galilee, and manifested his glory. And his disciples believed in him." John 2:11

Additional Reading: John 2:1–12

FRIDAY

"A bright cloud overshadowed them, and a voice from the cloud said, 'This is my beloved Son, with whom I am well pleased; listen to him.' When the disciples heard this, they fell on their faces and were terrified. But Jesus came and touched them, saying, 'Rise, and have no fear.' And when they lifted up their eyes, they saw no one but Jesus only." Matthew 17:5–8

Additional Reading: Matthew 17:1–9

Open Intercession or Daily Intercession

For daily intercessions see Appendix F.

Prayer for the Week

O good Jesus, Word of the Father and brightness of his glory, whom angels desire to behold, teach me to do your will that, guided by your Spirit, I may come to that blessed city of everlasting day, where all are one in heart and mind, where there is safety and eternal peace, happiness and delight, where you live with the Father and the Holy Spirit, world without end. *Amen. —Based on a prayer of St. Gregory*

Song for the Season

Sing a song of your choice.

 EPIPHANY—SECOND WEEK AFTER CHRISTMAS

The Lighting of the Candle

The leader prays as a participant lights the Christ candle.

LEADER Let us pray. Lord Jesus, may your light shine our way. Lead us by your presence that we may love and worship you in all things.

Meditation or Silence

After a moment of silence or a physical expression of prayer, the leader continues.

LEADER Jesus, there is healing in your presence.

Psalm

MONDAY • Psalm 29:1–11 **TUESDAY** • Psalm 44:1–8 **WEDNESDAY** • Psalm 47:6–9
THURSDAY • Psalm 68:32–35 **FRIDAY** • Psalm 102:15–22

Song for the Season

Sing a song of your choice.

Short Verse

READER Jesus came proclaiming the Good News of God, saying, "The time is fulfilled, and the kingdom of God is at hand; repent and believe in the gospel." Mark 1:15

Short Prayer

READER   Jesus, grant us the wisdom to seek your kingdom in our daily lives.

Scripture Reading

EVERYONE   Father, open our eyes that we might see the wonders of your truth.

MONDAY

Jesus commissioned his disciples: "He sent them out to proclaim the kingdom of God and to heal." Luke 9:2

Additional Reading: Luke 9:1–6

TUESDAY

Jesus said: "Blessed are you who are poor, for yours is the kingdom of God." Luke 6:20

Additional Reading: Luke 6:20–23

WEDNESDAY

Jesus said: "Heaven and earth will pass away, but my words will not pass away." Matthew 24:35

Additional Reading: Matthew 24:32–36

THURSDAY

From the very beginning of his ministry to just before he ascended, Jesus spoke of the kingdom of God: "He presented himself alive to them after his suffering by many proofs, appearing to them during forty days and speaking about the kingdom of God." Acts 1:3

Additional Reading: Acts 1:1–5

FRIDAY

God has reconciled us through Christ and given us the ministry of reconciliation: "Therefore, we are ambassadors for Christ, God making his appeal through us. We implore you on behalf of Christ, be reconciled to God." 2 Corinthians 5:20

Additional Reading: 2 Corinthians 5:16–21

Open Intercession or Daily Intercession

For daily intercessions see Appendix F.

Prayer for the Week

Grant me, O Lord my God, a mind to know you, a heart to seek you, wisdom to find you, conduct pleasing to you, faithful perseverance in waiting for you, and a hope of finally embracing you. *Amen. —Based on a prayer of St. Thomas Aquinas*

Song for the Season

Sing a song of your choice.

 EPIPHANY—THIRD WEEK AFTER CHRISTMAS

The Lighting of the Candle

The leader prays as a participant lights the Christ candle.

LEADER   Let us pray. Lord Jesus, may your light shine our way. Lead us by your presence that we may love and worship you in all things.

Meditation or Silence

After a moment of silence or a physical expression of prayer, the leader continues.

LEADER   Jesus, may your love penetrate to the depths of our souls.

Psalm

MONDAY • Psalm 37:3–11   TUESDAY • Psalm 63:1–3   WEDNESDAY • Psalm 51:1–4, 10–17
THURSDAY • Psalm 13:20–22   FRIDAY • Psalm 119:41–48

Song for the Season

Sing a song of your choice.

Short Verse

READER   Jesus said: "Blessed are the peacemakers, for they shall be called sons of God." Matthew 5:9

Short Prayer

READER   Teacher, instruct me in the law of your love.

Scripture Reading

EVERYONE   Father, open our eyes that we might see the wonders of your truth.

MONDAY

Jesus said: "Do not think that I have come to abolish the Law or the Prophets; I have not come to abolish them but to fulfill them." Matthew 5:17

Additional Reading: Matthew 5:1–16

TUESDAY

Jesus gave a new commandment: "Love one another. As I have loved you, so you must love one another." John 13:34 (NIV)

Additional Reading: John 13:1–38

WEDNESDAY

For the whole law is fulfilled in one word: "You shall love your neighbor as yourself." Galatians 5:14

Additional Reading: Galatians 5:13–16

THURSDAY

God is the author of all good things in us: "O Lord, you will ordain peace for us, for you have indeed done for us all our works." Isaiah 26:12

Additional Reading: Isaiah 26:1–12

FRIDAY

"This is how we know that we love the children of God: by loving God and carrying out his commands." 1 John 5:2 (NIV)

Additional Reading: 1 John 5:1–5

Open Intercession or Daily Intercession

For daily intercessions see Appendix F.

Prayer for the Week

O Jesus, King of Glory, our eternal king and friend, your throne is fixed in heaven, your kingdom has no end: and now to all men, far and near, Lord, reveal it now, we pray, that as in heaven all creatures here may know you and obey. To you the morning star does lead; to you the Incarnate Word, we worship you, Savior, in our need; we worship you, our Lord. Amen. —*Based on "O Jesu, King of Glory," by Martin Boehme*

Song for the Season ✠
Sing a song of your choice.

The Lighting of the Candle

The leader prays as a participant lights the Christ candle.

LEADER Let us pray. Lord Jesus, may your light shine our way. Lead us by your presence that we may love and worship you in all things.

Meditation or Silence

After a moment of silence or a physical expression of prayer, the leader continues.

LEADER Father, you bring us perfect peace.

Psalm

MONDAY • Psalm 119:1–8   TUESDAY • Psalm 119:17–24   WEDNESDAY • Psalm 119:25–32
THURSDAY • Psalm 119:33–40   FRIDAY • Psalm 119:73–80

Song for the Season

Sing a song of your choice.

Short Verse

READER And Jesus said to them, "Follow me, and I will make you become fishers of men." Mark 1:17

Short Prayer

READER Lord, give me the faith to leave my desires and follow you.

Scripture Reading

EVERYONE Father, open our eyes that we might see the wonders of your truth.

MONDAY

Jesus said: "Come, follow me," and they dropped everything to follow him. Matthew 4:19–20 (NIV)

Additional Reading: Matthew 4:18–22

TUESDAY

Jesus said: "No one who puts his hand to the plow and looks back is fit for service in the kingdom of God." Luke 9:62

Additional Reading: Luke 9:57–62

WEDNESDAY

Jesus said: "Whoever does the will of my Father in heaven is my brother and sister and mother." Matthew 12:50

Additional Reading: Matthew 12:46–50

THURSDAY

Jesus said: "If anyone would come after me, let him deny himself and take up his cross daily and follow me." Luke 9:23

Additional Reading: Luke 9:23–27

FRIDAY

Jesus understood the rich young ruler and knew what kept him from the Kingdom: "Sell your possessions and give to the poor, and you will have treasure in heaven. Then come, follow me." Matthew 19:21 (NIV)

Additional Reading: Matthew 19:16–30

Open Intercession or Daily Intercession
For daily intercessions see Appendix F.

Prayer for the Week

Take, O Lord, and receive my entire liberty, my memory, my understanding, and my whole will. All that I am and all that I possess, you have given me. I surrender it all to you to be disposed of according to your will. Give me only your love and your grace; with these I will be rich enough, and will desire nothing more. *Amen.*
—*Based on a prayer of St. Ignatius of Loyola*

Song for the Season ✠
Sing a song of your choice.

The Lighting of the Candle

The leader prays as a participant lights the candle.[21]

LEADER   Let us pray. Jesus, Light of the World, illumine us with your presence.

Meditation or Silence ☦

After a moment of silence or a physical expression of prayer, the leader continues.

LEADER   Father, we are humbled in your holy presence.

Psalm

MONDAY • Psalm 25:6–9   TUESDAY • Psalm 18:27–32   WEDNESDAY • Psalm 147:5–11

THURSDAY • Psalm 34:1–5   FRIDAY • Psalm 149:1–4

Song for the Season ☦

Sing a song of your choice.

Short Verse

READER   Peter wrote: "Clothe yourselves, all of you, with humility toward one
another, for 'God opposes the proud but gives grace to the humble.'"
1 Peter 5:5

Short Prayer

READER   Son of God, give to me a humble heart prepared to serve.

Scripture Reading

EVERYONE   Father, open our eyes that we might see the wonders of your truth.

MONDAY

Isaiah saw the Lord in all his majesty. As the angels worshiped God, Isaiah recognized his sinfulness: "Woe is me! For I am lost; for I am a man of unclean lips, and I
dwell in the midst of a people of unclean lips." Isaiah 6:5

Additional Reading: Isaiah 6:1–7

TUESDAY

The prophet Zechariah wrote: "See, your king comes to you, righteous and having
salvation, gentle and riding on a donkey." Zechariah 9:9 (NIV)

Additional Reading: Zechariah 9:9; Matthew 21:5

WEDNESDAY

Even though he was their master and teacher, he humbled himself to wash the feet of his disciples: "Unless I wash you, you have no part with me." John 13:8 (NIV)

Additional Reading: John 13:1–20

THURSDAY

Jesus said: "For even the Son of Man came not to be served but to serve, and to give his life as a ransom for many." Mark 10:45

Additional Reading: Mark 10:42–45

FRIDAY

Paul wrote of Christ our Lord: "And being found in human form, he humbled himself by becoming obedient to the point of death, even death on a cross." Philippians 2:8

Additional Reading: Philippians 2:5–11

Open Intercession or Daily Intercession
For daily intercessions see Appendix F.

Prayer for the Week

O Jesus,
Humble of heart, hear me.
From the desire of being esteemed, deliver me, O Jesus.
From the desire of being loved,
From the desire of being honored,
From the desire of being praised,
From the desire of being preferred to others,
From the desire of being consulted,
From the desire of being approved.
Jesus, place in me the same attitude as you, considering myself nothing. May only God, our Father, exalt me. *Amen.*

—Based on a prayer of Rafael Merry del Val

Song for the Season ✠
Sing a song of your choice.

Note: If Lent begins this week, these liturgies should begin this week. On Wednesday, the liturgies should transition to the liturgy for Ash Wednesday, which is located on page 97.[22]

The Lighting of the Candle

The leader prays as a participant lights the candle.

LEADER   Let us pray. Jesus, Light of the World, illumine us with your presence.

Meditation or Silence ✚

After a moment of silence or a physical expression of prayer, the leader continues.

LEADER   Jesus, in your grace I am free and at peace.

Psalm

MONDAY • Psalm 17:6–8   TUESDAY • Psalm 98:1–4   WEDNESDAY • Psalm 119:25–32
THURSDAY • Psalm 36:5–9   FRIDAY • Psalm 42:1–8

Song for the Season ✚

Sing a song of your choice.

Short Verse

READER   Paul wrote: "For by grace you have been saved through faith. And this is not your own doing; it is the gift of God." Ephesians 2:8

Short Prayer

READER   Savior, let me extend grace as you have given grace to me.

Scripture Reading

EVERYONE   Father, open our eyes that we might see the wonders of your truth.

MONDAY

From Abraham to us today, God's covenants always begin and end with his grace: "And [Abram] believed the LORD, and he counted it to him as righteousness." Genesis 15:6

Additional Reading: Genesis 12:1–3; Genesis 15:1–6

TUESDAY

Jacob prayed to God: "I am not worthy of the least of all the deeds of steadfast love and all the faithfulness that you have shown to your servant." Genesis 32:10

Additional Reading: Genesis 32:9–12

WEDNESDAY

Moses sang of God's great victory: "With your unfailing love you lead the people you have redeemed. In your might, you guide them to your sacred home." Exodus 15:13 (NLT)

Additional Reading: Exodus 15:11–18

THURSDAY

Even though his people were unfaithful, God promised: "I will betroth you to me forever. I will betroth you to me in righteousness and in justice, in steadfast love and in mercy." Hosea 2:19

Additional Reading: Hosea 2:16–23

FRIDAY

God's love is completely different from conditional love: "But God shows his love for us in that while we were still sinners, Christ died for us." Romans 5:8

Additional Reading: Romans 5:6–11

Open Intercession or Daily Intercession
For daily intercessions see Appendix F.

Prayer for the Week
O Lord, we ask you, pour your grace into our hearts;
You announced to us the Incarnation of Christ, your Son,
By the message of an angel so that
By his Passion and Cross,
We might be brought to the glory of his Resurrection
Through Jesus Christ our Lord. *Amen.*
—*Based on an excerpt from the Angelus*

Song for the Season
Sing a song of your choice.

Note: If Lent begins this week, these liturgies should begin this week. On Wednesday, the liturgies should transition to Ash Wednesday, which is located on page 97.[23]

The Lighting of the Candle

The leader prays as a participant lights the candle.

LEADER   Let us pray. Jesus, Light of the World, illumine us with your presence.

Meditation or Silence

After a moment of silence or a physical expression of prayer, the leader continues.

LEADER   Father, may our souls find rest in trusting you.

Psalm

MONDAY • Psalm 20:4–9   TUESDAY • Psalm 37:3–6   WEDNESDAY • Psalm 44:4–8

THURSDAY • Psalm 71:1–8   FRIDAY • Psalm 91:1–2

Song for the Season

Sing a song of your choice.

Short Verse

READER   "Without faith it is impossible to please [God]." Hebrews 11:6

Short Prayer

READER   Father, increase my faith that I may gain understanding.

Scripture Reading

EVERYONE   Father, open our eyes that we might see the wonders of your truth.

MONDAY

The righteous shall live by his faith. Habakkuk 2:4

Additional Reading: Habakkuk 2:1–5

TUESDAY

Though Abraham did not understand fully, he believed that God would return Isaac. He said: "I and the boy will go over there and worship and come again to you." Genesis 22:5

Additional Reading: Genesis 22:1–8

WEDNESDAY

Rahab did not have heritage or morality to justify her before God. But she did have faith, and it saved her and her entire family: "When the LORD gives us the land we will deal kindly and faithfully with you." Joshua 2:14

Additional Reading: Joshua 2:1–14

THURSDAY

Abraham's standing with God had nothing to do with the law or his works. His righteousness came only by faith: "Abraham believed God, and it was counted to him as righteousness." Romans 4:3

Additional Reading: Romans 4:1–3, 20–25

FRIDAY

Throughout history, people from diverse backgrounds and situations have been commended for their faith: "Now faith is being sure of what we hope for and certain of what we do not see. This is what the ancients were commended for." Hebrews 11:1–2 (NIV)

Additional Reading: Hebrews 11:13–22

Open Intercession or Daily Intercession
For daily intercessions see Appendix F.

Prayer for the Week

We acknowledge, O Lord, and give thanks that you have created us in your image, so that we might remember you, think of you, and love you. But this image is so worn away by the fall, it is so obscured by our sins, that we cannot do what we were created to do, unless you renew and reform us. We are not attempting, O Lord, to penetrate your loftiness, for we cannot begin to match our understanding with it, but we desire in some measure to understand your truth, which our hearts believe and love. For we do not seek to understand in order that we might believe, but we believe in order to understand. For this, too, we believe, that unless we believe, we will not understand. *Amen. —Based on a prayer of St. Anselm*

Song for the Season ✠
Sing a song of your choice.

67

Note: If Lent begins this week, these liturgies should begin this week. On Wednesday, the liturgies should transition to Ash Wednesday, which is located on page 97.[24]

The Lighting of the Candle
The leader prays as a participant lights the candle.
LEADER Let us pray. Jesus, Light of the World, illumine us with your presence.

Meditation or Silence ✝
After a moment of silence or a physical expression of prayer, the leader continues.
LEADER Father, we come clothed in Christ, free and confident in your presence.

Psalm
MONDAY • Psalm 69:6; 13–18 **TUESDAY** • Psalm 42:11 **WEDNESDAY** • Psalm 130:1–8
THURSDAY • Psalm 146:1–7 **FRIDAY** • Psalm 9:9–10, 18

Song for the Season ✝
Sing a song of your choice.

Short Verse
READER The apostle Paul wrote: "God chose to make known how great among the Gentiles are the riches of the glory of this mystery, which is Christ in you, the hope of glory." Colossians 1:27

Short Prayer
READER Lord Jesus Christ, let me never be put to shame.

Scripture Reading
EVERYONE Father, open our eyes that we might see the wonders of your truth.

MONDAY

God told Joshua: "Be strong and courageous. Do not be terrified; do not be discouraged, for the LORD your God will be with you wherever you go." Joshua 1:9 (NIV)

Additional Reading: Joshua 1:1–9

TUESDAY

Jeremiah recounted that only God was powerful enough to provide and protect: "We set our hope on you." Jeremiah 14:22

Additional Reading: Jeremiah 14:17–22

WEDNESDAY

The Lord spoke to Jeremiah: "Blessed is the man who trusts in the LORD, whose confidence is in him." Jeremiah 17:7 (NIV)

Additional Reading: Jeremiah 17:5–8

THURSDAY

God encouraged his people: "For I know the plans I have for you, declares the LORD, plans for welfare and not for evil, to give you a future and a hope." Jeremiah 29:11

Additional Reading: Jeremiah 29:1–14

FRIDAY

The apostle Paul writes: "Rejoice in hope, be patient in tribulation, be constant in prayer." Romans 12:12

Additional Reading: Romans 12:1–12

Open Intercession or Daily Intercession
For daily intercessions see Appendix F.

Prayer for the Week

We have heard and we know that you are the everlasting God, the Creator of the ends of the earth. You do not faint or grow weary; your understanding is unsearchable. You give power to the weak, and to us who have no might, you increase our strength. Even the youth faint and grow weary, and the young men fall exhausted. But we wait for you, Lord, and believe that you shall renew our strength. We will mount up with wings like eagles; we will run and not be weary; we will walk and not faint. Amen. —*Prayer based on the text of Isaiah* 40:28–31

Song for the Season ✚
Sing a song of your choice.

Note: Lent begins this week. On Wednesday transition to the Ash Wednesday liturgies on page 97.[25]

The Lighting of the Candle

The leader prays as a participant lights the candle.

LEADER   Let us pray. Jesus, Light of the World, illumine us with your presence.

Meditation or Silence

After a moment of silence or a physical expression of prayer, the leader continues.

LEADER   To whom else could we go? Jesus, you have the words of eternal life.

Psalm

MONDAY • Psalm 145:1–9   **TUESDAY** • Psalm 146:1–10   **WEDNESDAY** • Psalm 147:1–6
THURSDAY • Psalm 148:1–6   **FRIDAY** • Psalm 149:1–4

Song for the Season

Sing a song of your choice.

Short Verse

READER   "Greater love has no one than this, that someone lay down his life for his friends." John 15:13

Short Prayer

READER   Jesus, my Savior, teach me to love as you love.

Scripture Readings

EVERYONE   Father, open our eyes that we might see the wonders of your truth.

MONDAY

Both the Torah and Jesus teach us: "Love your neighbor as yourself." Leviticus 19:18
Additional Reading: Leviticus 19:9–18

TUESDAY

"For I am sure that neither death nor life, nor angels nor rulers, nor things present nor things to come, nor powers, nor height nor depth, nor anything else in all creation, will be able to separate us from the love of God in Christ Jesus our Lord." Romans 8:38–39
Additional Reading: John 15:12–17

Note: See the liturgy for Ash Wednesday, in the First Week of Lent on page 97.

Open Intercession or Daily Intercession
For daily intercessions see Appendix F.

Prayer for the Week

Almighty and everlasting God, in your tender love for your creation you sent your son, our Savior Jesus Christ, to take upon himself our nature, to suffer death upon the cross. Mercifully grant that we might also walk in that self-sacrificing love, even if it means we must share in his suffering. Amen. *—Based on a collect from the Book of Common Prayer*

Song for the Season ✠
Sing a song of your choice.

(or Before the Christmas Meal)

The Lighting of the Christ Candle on Christmas

LEADER Father, today we celebrate with complete joy the birth of your Son, our Lord, Jesus Christ, who is the Light of the World.

Special Reading for Christmas Day

Christmas Day marks the beginning of the Twelve Days of Christmas and opens with a fine meal and a simple reading:

READER On the Morning of Christ's Nativity
This is the month, and this the happy morn
Where the Son of Heaven's eternal King,
Of wedded Maid, and Virgin Mother born,
Our great redemption from above did bring;
For so the holy sages once did sing,
That he our deadly forfeit should release,
And with his Father work us a perpetual peace.
—*From "On the Morning of Christ's Nativity," by John Milton*

Song
"Joy to the World"

Prayer on Christmas Day

LEADER The day of your birth resembles you, Lord, because it brings joy to all humanity. Old people and infants alike enjoy this day. Your day is celebrated from generation to generation. In the winter when trees are bare, you give us the most succulent spiritual fruit. In the frost when the earth is barren, you bring new hope to our souls. In December when seeds are hidden in the soil, the staff of life springs forth from the virgin womb. Amen. —*Based on a prayer of St. Ephraim the Syrian (AD 306–373)*

Reading from the Scriptures

READER "For unto you is born this day in the city of David a Savior, who is Christ the Lord." Luke 2:11
Additional Reading: Luke 2:1–21

Depending on the time this liturgy is used, the family may open gifts or celebrate a fine family meal afterward.

The Celebration of the King

The special dinner and liturgy for the winter season is called *The Celebration of the King*. This celebration commemorates Christ's birth, the visit of the Magi, Jesus' baptism, and his first miracle. Historically, the church has centered the celebration upon Christ's baptism, drawing attention to the beginning of his ministry.

PREPARING FOR *The Celebration of the King*

DECORATIONS ✠ During the Advent and Christmas seasons, the family may make symbols that can be reincorporated for this home gathering. These images or symbols can be used to decorate the walls or the table. Some symbols of particular importance for this liturgy are:

> Three ivory pillar candles
> Basin of water and a white towel
> Smaller taper candle and candle stand for each participant

FOOD ✠ This celebration is designed to feel like a feast or a banquet. The liturgy revolves around the food and the symbols on the table. Therefore, you may wish to place all the food on the table at the beginning of the meal, rather than bringing it out in courses. Also, the food should be served family style to encourage interaction and a spirit of community. Since food is a key component of the liturgy, elegant presentation may enhance the overall experience. The foods of particular importance for this home gathering are:

> A fish entrée[26]
> Loaf of bread
> Red wine (or grape juice)
> Plates of grapes
> Sparkling cider or champagne
> A King's Cake, which may be purchased or baked[27]

SCAVENGER HUNT If children are present, a simple scavenger hunt can officially begin the evening. Hiding a few elements around the house represents the hidden traces of Jesus Christ throughout the Old Testament. The symbols for the scavenger hunt are:

One box or container of seeds, representing the Seed of Redemption
Several small sticks or rods, representing the staff of the prophets
One paper or toy crown, representing the crown of a king
One bottle of oil, representing the anointing of the Priest

READERS The host may select the readers prior to the meal.

LITURGY FOR

The Celebration of the King

Welcome to the Celebration

If children are present, the liturgy begins here. For older groups, see page 74.

LEADER Welcome to *The Celebration of the King*. We begin our celebration by discovering the symbols of Jesus Christ throughout the house. The entire Old Testament looks forward to Jesus Christ. From creation to the fall, through the Exodus and through the kingdoms, the entire Old Testament and all of redemptive history anticipate its fulfillment in Jesus Christ. Just as the prophecies are scattered throughout the entire Old Testament, the scavenger hunt items are scattered throughout the house. These are the items you need to find:

One box of large seeds
Several small wooden rods or sticks[28]
One crown
One bottle of oil

Allow a few minutes for the children to find the items listed above.

LEADER God likes to hide things so that he can reveal them to people who have faith. Over thousands of years, God provided clues for his people so that they would anticipate the fulfillment of all things in his Son, Jesus.

Who found the box of seeds?

The child who found the box of seeds brings it to the leader.

These seeds represent that the serpent and his seed would be at war with the seed of the woman, Eve. Early in Genesis, God promises that the Messiah will ultimately crush evil, but it will cost him his life. The prophecy is unclear because it is a long way from its fulfillment. We do not know who the Messiah is or where he comes from. We do not know how he will defeat evil. But as history progresses the prophecies concerning the Messiah get clearer and clearer.

Who found a stick?

Children who found sticks bring them to the leader.

We use these sticks to symbolize a prophet's staff. For thousands of years, prophets told of the Messiah who was coming. Some prophets were well educated. Others were poor shepherds. Some prophesied more than a thousand years before Christ's birth. Others were closer in time. No matter their education or their time, they all pointed to Jesus as the coming Messiah.

Who found the crown?

The child who found the crown brings it to the leader.

The promise is given throughout the Old Testament that a new King will come to establish the peaceable kingdom of God. God made the promise clear to his great King David: "I will set him over my house and my kingdom forever; his throne will be established forever."

Who found the bottle of oil?

The child who found the bottle brings it to the leader.

The bottle of oil symbolizes that Jesus is the Great High Priest. He is the only one who is able to mediate between God and us, once for all. Jesus alone brings us peace with God.

The Lighting of the First Candle—A Light to the Nations

If the group is older, the scavenger hunt may be omitted, and the liturgy begins here.

A participant lights the first white pillar candle.

LEADER   On this day, we celebrate the birth, life, and ministry of Jesus, who is the fulfillment of all the Scriptures and all of redemptive history. He came to redeem us from the Fall and restore us to God. Jesus is the "Light of the Nations." The prophet Isaiah said, "The people walking in darkness have seen a great light."

EVERYONE Jesus was born to become a light to enlighten the nations and the glory of God's people, Israel. Glory to God the Father, God the Son, and God the Holy Spirit. As it was in the beginning, is now, and so shall be forever. *Amen.*

Song for the Season ✚
Sing a song of your choice.

The Breaking of Bread
LEADER The Wise Men followed the star to the city of David, which is Bethlehem, which means "the house of bread." There they found the one who would be the "Bread of Life." Tonight as we break the bread, we remember the three kings who followed the star to find the King of Kings.

The Basin of Water—Jesus' Baptism
As the participants continue to eat and converse, a reader gathers everyone's attention.

READER When all the people were being baptized, Jesus was baptized, as well. As he was praying, heaven opened and the Holy Spirit descended on him like a dove. A voice came from heaven: "You are my Son, whom I love; with you I am well pleased."

LEADER Jesus' baptism explains to us the essence of the divine life—submission to the Holy Spirit to the pleasure of God the Father. In his baptism, Jesus submits himself to the Spirit, and the Triune God reveals the power of loving, mutual submission.

READER Baptism is an emptying of ourselves in exchange for God's life. We are enlightened in order to radiate light; we are clothed, taking away all our shame; we are bathed because it washes us clean; and we are sealed, as it is our guard and the sign of God's lordship in our lives.[29]

LEADER: Let us wash our hands in the water, reminding us of our baptism. In this act, we restate our submission to the Spirit and our desires to live the divine life he gives.

Each participant washes his or her hands and dries them.

The New Covenant
As the participants continue to eat and converse, a reader gathers everyone's attention.

READER Jesus said to the servants, "Fill the jars with water"; so they filled them to the brim. Then he told them, "Now draw some out and take it to the master of the banquet." They did, and the master of the banquet tasted the water. It had been turned into wine. Then he called the bridegroom aside and said, "Everyone brings out the choice wine first and then the cheaper wine after the guests have had too much to drink; but you have saved the best till now."

LEADER   Jesus' miracle was a symbol of the wine of the new and everlasting covenant. The abundance of wine provided for this wedding feast represents the overabundance of God's grace and love. Finally, it looks forward to the feast of the great wedding banquet of the Lamb, the celebration of the completion of God's redemption of the world. *The leader fills everyone's cup with red wine. For those who do not drink alcohol or for children, a pitcher of sparkling grape juice may be provided.*

The True Vine
As the participants continue to eat and converse, the reader takes a bundle of grapes, gathers everyone's attention, and reads.

READER   Jesus said, "I am the vine; you are the branches. If you remain in me and I in you, you will bear much fruit. But, apart from me you can do nothing."

LEADER   Jesus promises a new life. No longer are we relegated to live in our fallen existence. When we abide in him, Jesus gives us new life filled with his love. Jesus said, "My command is this: Love each other as I have loved you. Greater love has no one than this, that he lay down his life for his friends." As we abide in the vine, may the sweet taste of the fruit of God's love exude from our lives.

The leader encourages the participants to enjoy the grapes.

Second Candle—The Light of the World
The reader lights the second white pillar candle and reads.

READER   The second candle that we light tonight is the "Light of the World." Jesus said, "I am the Light of the world; whoever walks with me will not walk in darkness but will have the light of life."

LEADER   Look around and see the lights on this table and remember the words of our Savior. Not only is he the Light of the World, but also he has made us to be the light of the world. Jesus also said: "You are the light of the world." Everyone, take your unlit candle and light it from the second pillar candle. As we live in Christ, we too become the light of the world. *Everyone takes the taper candles and lights them from the second pillar candle.*

Song for the Season ✠
Sing a song of your choice.

Call of Jesus' Disciples

As the participants continue to eat and converse, a reader gathers everyone's attention.

READER When Jesus begins his ministry, he announces: "The time has come. The kingdom of God is near. Repent and believe the good news!"

LEADER When Jesus calls his disciples, he calls them to drop everything and follow him. He calls them to be fishers of men. The next symbol is the fish that we are eating for dinner. The current of the world tries to pull us into its ways of life, but as believers, we must resist and live the powerful truth of the gospel, even though it may require us to swim upstream.

Third Candle—Transfiguration

LEADER This season we celebrate the incarnation of God in Jesus Christ. At his baptism, Jesus demonstrates his humanity. But at the mount of transfiguration, Jesus unveils his glory, revealing that he is the fullness of God. A bright cloud envelops everyone who is present, and when Peter, James, and John look up, Moses and Elijah are no longer there. They see no one except Jesus.

READER God, before the Passion of your only-begotten Son, he revealed his glory upon the holy mountain. Give to us your servants the faith to see the light of his face, that we may be strengthened to daily bear our cross, and be changed into his likeness from glory to glory; through Jesus Christ our Lord. *Amen.*[30]

A participant (if present, preferably a child) lights the third pillar.

The New Kingdom ✠

Finally, the King's Cake (which may be purchased or baked) is brought out by the host.[31]

LEADER Jesus came to establish a new kingdom, one that would last forever. The King's Cake reminds us not only of the small Child-King that the Magi attended, but also of the Great King, our returning champion, the rider on the white horse—Jesus Christ, the King of Kings and Lord of Lords.

A Toast to the King

After some time to eat the cake and drink some coffee, everyone fills his or her wine glass with champagne or sparkling cider, and the leader makes a toast.

LEADER We conclude our time together with one final toast and raise our glasses to the King, to celebrate his life and his victory. To the King!

EVERYONE To the King!

Preparing for the Season   81

✠ *This symbol denotes that additional resources or reminders may be found at the athomewithgod.org website.*

Preparing for the Season

Spring 🌸

Out of the depths of winter comes the new life of spring. The season itself tells the story of death and resurrection and is captured in the liturgical calendar. The three focal points of spring are:

LENT—a time of reflection and sacrifice, the path to the cross

EASTER—celebrating Jesus' resurrection and new life

FROM EASTER TO PENTECOST—awaiting the Holy Spirit

Lent

Lent, like Advent, is a season of preparation. This season begins on Ash Wednesday and marks Jesus' road to the cross. During this season, we focus on God's desire to set his people free from bondage. The biblical story centers around the liberation of God's people in the work of Jesus, our Passover Lamb. Therefore, the Exodus story undergirds the readings during the Lenten season and anticipates the sacrifice of Jesus for our salvation. For the date for the beginning of Lent, see Appendix B on page 239 or register at the athomewithgod.org website to receive seasonal and date reminders.

Easter

Easter is the great celebration of Christ's atonement for our sins and his resurrection from the grave. This time of year is one of the most joyous, celebrating the resurrection of our Lord. During Easter, families or home groups may celebrate the home gathering of *The Celebration of Redemption*, which is an adapted and "fulfilled" Passover Seder.[32] Maundy Thursday (the Thursday immediately preceding Easter) is the ideal time for *The Celebration of Redemption*.

From Easter to Pentecost

The day after Easter begins the path to Pentecost, which is exactly fifty days from Easter. This time shifts its focus from our delivery from bondage to the liberty of new life. Passover celebrates our freedom *from* bondage; Pentecost celebrates our freedom *to* live as God's people.

This season anticipates the presence of the Holy Spirit, who provides for us freedom in Christ and a new life.

Traditions for the Season

SPECIAL ACTIVITIES

ASH WEDNESDAY AND THE LENTEN FAST Ash Wednesday marks the beginning of the season of Lent.[33] The prominent symbol of Ash Wednesday is, of course, the ashes. Many local parishes or congregations mark parishioners with a cross of ashes upon the forehead.

During Lent, families or home groups may abstain from certain luxuries or foods. Historically, abstaining from food has been the primary source of fasting. Fasting from certain food reminds us that man does not live by bread alone, but by every word that comes from God's mouth. Fasting is also a reminder to crave and savor God's voice in our lives. In addition, fasting is how Jesus began his ministry. He was led into the wilderness by the Spirit. Often, the wilderness is where we truly learn to listen and depend on God.

Another home tradition for Lent is giving and serving in a way so that we are not seen (which is a direct reference to the first reading of the season in Matthew 6). This may include covertly or secretly blessing other people by giving gifts or performing acts of service.

HOLY WEEK AND EASTER LITURGIES Holy Week is the week prior to Easter beginning on Palm Sunday. This time marks the progression from Jesus' triumphal entry into the city of Jerusalem (Palm Sunday), to his betrayal, the Last Supper, his crucifixion, and, ultimately, his resurrection.

This week, families or home groups may employ special liturgies in anticipation of Easter Sunday. The liturgy shown below includes seven candles, one for each day leading to Easter. Each night all the candles are lit and then a certain number of candles are extinguished for each night. Finally, the Saturday night before Easter, all the candles are extinguished and the opening of Sabbath is *not* celebrated. This Saturday is the only opening of Sabbath that is not celebrated in the church year. On Holy Saturday, we use darkness and the absence of

Sabbath to feel the weight of the loss suffered on the cross, and remind ourselves of the despair of the disciples during this time.

SPECIAL SYMBOLS FOR THE SEASON ✚

Below is a list of signs and symbols that could be used for these seasons.

PURPLE OR LAVENDER—DURING LENT Purple or lavender are the traditional liturgical colors for the Lenten Season and are associated with humility and modesty.

WHITE OR GOLD—EASTER White and gold are celebratory colors representing purity and the newness of life that comes from victory over sin and death. In addition, these colors represent the illumination of the risen Christ.

GREEN—SPRING ORDINARY TIME Green is used during the "ordinary" times of the year and is a symbol of life and growth.

VEGETABLE SOUPS OR OTHER HUMBLE MEALS—DURING LENT ✚ Lent is a season of abstinence and discipline. We use humble, rustic dishes such as minestrone, potato soup, or lentil soup to accentuate this season as a time of self-denial.

FISH—DURING LENT The early church omitted meat from their diet because it was associated with plenty and luxury. Therefore, fish has been associated with fasting during this season.

LAVENDER—DURING LENT Lavender is associated with the preparation of Jesus' death and is associated with humility and self-sacrifice. In John 12, Mary pours "nard," the ancient Greek name for lavender, on Jesus' feet. Families may want to incorporate lavender tea, essential oils, or incense to associate the flavor or aroma with this season.

LAMB—DURING EASTER The symbolism of the sacrificial Lamb is ancient and rich and represents the atonement for and redemption of God's people. The symbol has its roots in the Exodus of God's people and the first night of Passover. By dying on the cross, Jesus is the Lamb of God who takes away the sins of the world, or as Paul writes in 1 Corinthians, "Christ our Passover has been sacrificed for us." Families or home groups may want to use lamb as the main course for *The Celebration of Redemption* and may also use the image of a lamb in arts, crafts, or decorations.

EASTER LILIES—DURING EASTER

The large white blossoms of the Easter lilies symbolize Jesus' purity and the illumination of his resurrection.

HOME GATHERING

THE CELEBRATION OF REDEMPTION The home gathering for this season is an adaptation of the Passover Seder. This liturgy is most likely the oldest surviving liturgy of the Christian faith. Though the liturgy remains true to its Hebrew roots, it is adapted for today's culture and expresses Messianic fulfillment in Jesus Christ and a celebration of his resurrection. Families or home groups are encouraged to host this celebration on Maundy Thursday.

The Lighting of the Candle

LEADER   Father, the light of your truth brings sight to the blindness of our sinful eyes. May this season of repentance bring us the blessing of your forgiveness and the gift of your light.

A participant lights the candle for the season.[34]

MEMBER   We praise you, God, King of the Universe, for you have given us Jesus Christ, the Light for those walking in darkness.

EVERYONE   We praise you, God, Creator and Redeemer.

LEADER   We praise you, God, King of the Universe, for you have given us this day of rest. During this season, Father, remind us of our own inadequacy. By losing our lives for your sake, may we gain the new life for which you created us. *Amen.*

The Blessing

Families with children may want to insert a short prayer for each child here.

LEADER   May the God of freedom enlighten us with his word, that we might cherish and savor his voice and deepen our commitment to follow him.

Song of Blessing ✠

The Lord bless you and keep you;
The Lord make his face shine upon you.
The Lord be gracious to you.
And give you his peace, forever.

Telling the Redemptive Story

The questions below are designed for children. Older groups may omit them.

LEADER   Why do we observe Lent?

CHILDREN   To remind us of Jesus' path to the cross.

LEADER   Why did Jesus have to die?

CHILDREN   To reconcile our fallen lives to a Holy God.

LEADER   Why do we fast during Lent?

CHILDREN   To remind us that in emptying ourselves we might receive new life in Jesus.

LEADER   Why do we not fast today?

CHILDREN   Every Sabbath, we remember that Jesus has made our salvation complete.

LEADER   Because Jesus is both the perfect sacrifice and the great high priest, we are free to enjoy his rest.

If the questions are omitted, the liturgy continues here.

LEADER   This season, we focus on the importance of the cross and Jesus' sacrifice. We also remember that Jesus asked us to take up our crosses daily— not that we live an oppressed life, rather, that we would lay down our lives to receive the new life that he freely gives.

All who are weary and burdened, come to Jesus and find your rest.

Readings for the Season ✠

FIRST WEEK OF LENT[35]

We enter this season with a humble heart before God: "O Lᴏʀᴅ, you have searched me and you know me. You know when I sit and when I rise; you perceive my thoughts from afar." Psalm 139:1–2

Additional Reading: Psalm 139
Weekday liturgies for this week are found on page 97.

SECOND WEEK OF LENT

We acknowledge our sin and ask for God's purity: "Create in me a pure heart, O God, and renew a steadfast spirit within me. . . . Restore to me the joy of your salvation and grant me a willing spirit, to sustain me." Psalm 51:10, 12 (ɴɪᴠ)

Additional Reading: Psalm 51
Weekday liturgies for this week are found on page 98.

THIRD WEEK OF LENT

With Paul, we restate our commitment and resolve: "For I resolved to know nothing while I was with you except Jesus Christ and him crucified."
I Corinthians 2:2 (ɴɪᴠ)

Additional Reading: 1 Corinthians 2:2–5
Weekday liturgies for this week are found on page 100.

FOURTH WEEK OF LENT

Paul believed that everything was worthless compared to knowing Christ Jesus: "But whatever was to my profit I now consider loss for the sake of Christ. What is more, I consider everything a loss compared to the surpassing greatness of knowing Christ Jesus my Lord." Philippians 3:7–8 (ɴɪᴠ)

Additional Reading: Philippians 3:7–11
Weekday liturgies for this week are found on page 102.

FIFTH WEEK OF LENT

Jesus knew that he must suffer to fulfill God's plan: "From that time on Jesus began to explain to his disciples that he must go to Jerusalem and suffer many things." Matthew 16:21 (NIV)

Additional Reading: Matthew 16:21–26
Weekday liturgies for this week are found on page 104.

SABBATH OF HOLY WEEK

Jesus entered the city of Jerusalem and the crowd shouted: "Hosanna to the Son of David! Blessed is he who comes in the name of the Lord! Hosanna in the highest!" Matthew 21:9

Additional Reading: Matthew 21:1–11
Weekday liturgies for this week are found on page 106.

ADDITIONAL Over dinner, older groups may want to engage in creative, explorative discussion of the Scriptures, in the ancient tradition of Midrash. See Appendix E.

Blessing the Cup

LEADER We praise you, God, King of the Universe, for you have given us the fruit of the vine. Father, you sent your son, Jesus, to be the Passover Lamb, to shed his blood for our salvation.

The leader pours the wine or juice and passes the cup so everyone drinks.

Blessing the Bread and Oil

LEADER We praise you, God, King of the Universe, for you give us bread from the earth. Jesus, you told us no one takes your life, but you lay it down. You willingly sacrificed your body for us.

LEADER We also praise you, God, King of the Universe, for you give us this oil. Spirit, Jesus promised that you would remind us of his teachings and counsel us in his ways. Tune our ears and teach us to listen to you.

EVERYONE We celebrate the birth, life, death, resurrection, ascension, and return of our King, Jesus Christ.

Everyone takes the bread, dips into the oil, and eats.

LEADER During this season of Lent, Father, we ask that you would dispel the darkness of sin and enlighten our hearts. May the symbols of this season remind us of Christ's sacrifice for the salvation and restoration of the world.

Song of Celebration

Sing a song of your choice.

The Peace of Sabbath

LEADER   The peace of Christ be with you.

EVERYONE   And also with you.

All pass the peace of Christ.

THE CLOSING OF SABBATH FOR LENT

The Greeting

LEADER   The Lord be with you.

EVERYONE   And also with you.

LEADER   When we are together, the Christ in me sees the Christ in you. Wherever we go, whatever we do, the ground we walk together is holy ground.

The Lighting of the Two Candles

The questions below are designed for children. Older groups may omit them.

LEADER   We part from the Sabbath ceremoniously, just as we welcomed it. This evening, we tell the conclusion of God's redemptive plan and celebrate our hope in its completion.

LEADER   What do the two candles symbolize?

CHILDREN   God has separated the holy from the common things.

LEADER   What has God set apart?

CHILDREN   God has set apart his people.

If the questions are omitted, the liturgy continues here.

LEADER   Just as God has set apart the Sabbath in order to bless the working week, God has also set apart his people. He has called out his people, the church, to bless, redeem, and restore the fallen world.

LEADER   We praise you, God, King of the Universe, who created light and set apart his people to be holy as you are holy.

One of the participants lights the two candles.

Song for the Season

Sing a song of your choice.

The Cup of Blessing

The leader lifts the cup for all to see.

LEADER We lift up the cup of salvation.

EVERYONE For salvation belongs to our God.

LEADER Father, your blessing be upon us now and forever.

The leader places the cup in a dish.

LEADER We praise you, God, King of the Universe, for you have given us the fruit of the vine and you generously pour out your blessing on us.

EVERYONE Fill our cups to overflowing.

LEADER May the blessing that you pour on us spill over into the lives of those around us.

A participant places the cup in a dish and fills the cup until it overflows, then pours the remaining wine or juice into a cup for each member.

Short Prayer for the Week

LEADER Though we know the truth of God's redemptive story, we often forget God. We become so accustomed to the world around us that we often blend in without thinking. These short prayers reconnect our spirits back to God's Spirit, asking him to tune our ears and refocus our attention to his work and our identity in Christ.

FIRST WEEK OF LENT
Kindle in my heart, O God, the flame of love that never ceases.

SECOND WEEK OF LENT
Lord Jesus Christ, fill me, I pray, with your light and life.[36]

THIRD WEEK OF LENT
O gracious and holy Father, give me wisdom to perceive you.[37]

FOURTH WEEK OF LENT
O gracious and holy Father, give me intelligence to understand you.

FIFTH WEEK OF LENT
O gracious and holy Father, give me diligence to seek you.

SABBATH OF HOLY WEEK
O gracious and holy Father, give me a heart to know you.

Conclusion of the Day of Rest

LEADER We now depart from our day of rest. Tomorrow we return to work even as we anticipate God's overflowing blessing on our lives this week. In returning to our work, we also long for our next day of rest as we long for the final day of rest, where we will enjoy a great banquet hosted by Jesus Christ our King.

MEMBER   God will prepare a feast with the best food and the greatest of aged wines.

LEADER   What do you think the great banquet will look like? What do you think we will eat? What will the music be like?

The participants imagine the great banquet.

A participant lights the incense and wafts it through the room.

LEADER   We praise you, God, King of the Universe, for you have given us our memories, our desires, and our senses. With great joy we remember the sweetness of this day of rest and anticipate the day of rest to come.

Blessing of the Week

LEADER   May the grace of Christ our Savior, the love of God our Father, and the fellowship of the Spirit be with us throughout this week and forevermore. *Amen.*

THE OPENING OF SABBATH FROM EASTER TO PENTECOST

The Lighting of the Candle

LEADER   Jesus said, "I am the resurrection and the life." Lord of life, light, and power, you have overcome death to make all things new.

A participant lights the candle for the season.[38]

MEMBER   We praise you, God, King of the Universe, for you have given us Jesus Christ, our Savior, the Resurrection and the Life.

EVERYONE   We praise you, God, Creator and Redeemer.

LEADER   We praise you, God, King of the Universe, for you have given us this day of rest. By Jesus' glorious resurrection you have delivered us from the power of our enemy. Allow us to die daily to sin, that we may enjoy you and the joy of his resurrection. May the light of your presence bless this home now and forever. *Amen.*

The Blessing

Families with children may want to insert a short prayer for each child here.

LEADER Spirit of the risen Christ, indwell this home and grant that we might live in new life and renewed hope because of your victory over the grave.

Song of Blessing ✠

The Lord bless you and keep you;
The Lord make his face shine upon you.
The Lord be gracious to you.
And give you his peace, forever.

Telling the Redemptive Story

The questions below are designed for children. Older groups may omit them.

LEADER What do we celebrate during this season?

CHILDREN Christ lived. Christ died. Christ rose again.

LEADER Why is it important that we believe that Christ rose from the dead?

CHILDREN If Christ is not raised, we have no hope. Our faith is meaningless.

LEADER How was Jesus raised from the dead?

CHILDREN God the Father raised him by the power of the Spirit.

LEADER The same Holy Spirit that raised Jesus from the dead lives in all who believe.

If the questions are omitted, the liturgy continues here.

LEADER This season we celebrate the joy of the resurrection. Jesus' resurrection not only gives us hope for a future resurrection, but also gives us new life on this earth by the power of the Holy Spirit. Because he is risen we have new life.

Readings for the Season ✠

RESURRECTION WEEK—THE WEEK FOLLOWING EASTER

On the third day, our risen Savior revealed himself while walking with the men on the road to Emmaus: "And beginning with Moses and all the Prophets, he explained to them what was said in all the Scriptures concerning himself." Luke 24:27 (NIV)

Additional Reading: Luke 24:13–35

Weekday liturgies for this week are found on page 115.

SIX WEEKS BEFORE PENTECOST

After his resurrection, Jesus spoke of the kingdom: "After his suffering, he showed himself to these men and gave many convincing proofs that he was alive. He appeared to them over a period of forty days and spoke about the kingdom of God." Acts 1:3

Additional Reading: Acts 1:1–8
Weekday liturgies for this week are found on page 117.

FIVE WEEKS BEFORE PENTECOST

Jesus told us of the coming Helper: "And I will ask the Father, and he will give you another Counselor, to be with you forever—the Spirit of truth. You know him, for he lives with you and will be in you. John 14:16–17 (NIV)

Additional Reading: John 14:15–26
Weekday liturgies for this week are found on page 119.

FOUR WEEKS BEFORE PENTECOST

Hundreds of years before the early church received the Spirit, the prophet Joel prophesied: "I will pour out my Spirit on all people. Your sons and daughters will prophesy, your old men will dream dreams, your young men will see visions. Even on my servants, both men and women, I will pour out my Spirit in those days." Joel 2:28–29 (NIV)

Additional Reading: Joel 2:24–29
Weekday liturgies for this week are found on page 121.

THREE WEEKS BEFORE PENTECOST

Jesus told his disciples: "It is for your good that I am going away. Unless I go away, the Counselor will not come to you; but if I go, I will send him to you." John 16:7 (NIV)

Additional Reading: John 16:5–16
Weekday liturgies for this week are found on page 123.

TWO WEEKS BEFORE PENTECOST

The Spirit is with the church from beginning to the end: "The Spirit and the Bride say, 'Come.' And let the one who hears say, 'Come.' And let the one who is thirsty come; let the one who desires take the water of life without price." Revelation 22:17

Additional Reading: Revelation 22:14–17
Weekday liturgies for this week are found on page 125.

THE WEEK BEFORE PENTECOST

Only the Holy Spirit can produce the fruit of the Spirit: "The fruit of the Spirit is love, joy, peace, patience, kindness, goodness, faithfulness, gentleness, self-control; against such things there is no law." Galatians 5:22–23

Additional Reading: Galatians 5:22–25
Weekday liturgies for this week are found on page 127.

ADDITIONAL Over dinner, older groups may want to engage in creative, explorative discussion of the Scriptures, in the ancient tradition of Midrash. See Appendix E.

Blessing the Cup

LEADER   We praise you, God, King of the Universe, for you have given us the fruit of the vine. Father, you sent your Son, who shed his blood to be the perfect sacrifice for our salvation.
The leader pours the wine or juice and passes the cup so everyone drinks.

Blessing the Bread and Oil

LEADER   We praise you, God, King of the Universe, for you give us bread from the earth. Jesus, you are the bread that came down from heaven. As you told us, he who believes will eat this bread and will live forever.

LEADER   We also praise you, God, King of the Universe, for you give us this oil. Spirit, you are the One who raised Jesus from the dead, and yet you live in us. You testify with our spirits that we are God's children.

EVERYONE   We celebrate the birth, life, death, resurrection, ascension, and return of our King, Jesus Christ.
Everyone takes the bread, dips into the oil, and eats.

LEADER   During this season, we ask that you would empower us to put to death the ways of the flesh and the world. Instead, let us live in accordance with the Spirit, the Spirit of peace.

Song of Celebration ✠
Sing a song of your choice.

The Peace of Sabbath

LEADER   The peace of Christ be with you.
EVERYONE   And also with you.
All pass the peace of Christ.

The Greeting

LEADER   The Lord be with you.

EVERYONE   And also with you.

LEADER   When we are together, the Christ in me sees the Christ in you. Wherever we go, whatever we do, the ground we walk together is holy ground.

The Lighting of the Two Candles

The questions below are designed for children. Older groups may omit them.

LEADER   We part from the Sabbath ceremoniously, just as we welcomed it. This evening, we tell the conclusion of God's redemptive plan and celebrate our hope in its completion.

LEADER   What do the two candles symbolize?

CHILDREN   God has separated the holy from the common things.

LEADER   What has God set apart?

CHILDREN   God has set apart his people.

If the questions are omitted, the liturgy continues here.

LEADER   Just as God has set apart the Sabbath in order to bless the working week, God has also set apart his people. He has called out his people, the church, to be a people of love. May the world know that we are followers of Jesus by the love we have for each other.

LEADER   We praise you God, King of the Universe, who created light. Spirit of the risen Christ, giver of life and light, empower us to experience and reveal the unsearchable depths of your love.

One of the participants lights the two candles.

Song for the Season ✚

Sing a song of your choice.

The Cup of Blessing

The leader lifts the cup for all to see.

LEADER   We lift up the cup of salvation.

EVERYONE   For salvation belongs to our God.

LEADER   Father, your blessing be upon us now and forever.

The leader places the cup in a dish.

LEADER   We praise you, God, King of the Universe, for you have given us the fruit of the vine and you generously pour out your blessing on us.

EVERYONE   Fill our cups to overflowing.

LEADER   May the blessing that you pour on us spill over into the lives of those around us.

A participant places the cup in a dish and fills the cup until it overflows, then pours the remaining wine or juice into a cup for each member.

Short Prayer for the Week

LEADER   Though we know the truth of God's redemptive story, we often forget God. We become so accustomed to the world around us that we often blend in without thinking. These short prayers reconnect our spirits back to God's Spirit, asking him to tune our ears and refocus our attention to his work and our identity in Christ.

RESURRECTION WEEK—THE WEEK FOLLOWING EASTER
Risen Christ, make us the living reality of God's presence.

SIX WEEKS BEFORE PENTECOST
Spirit of Truth, set us apart and renew our minds.

FIVE WEEKS BEFORE PENTECOST
Holy Spirit, awaken us from indifference. Give us active understanding.

FOUR WEEKS BEFORE PENTECOST
Good Counselor, indwell the deepest, inmost parts of our souls.

THREE WEEKS BEFORE PENTECOST
Spirit of Truth, give us faith to inquire, explore, and create.

TWO WEEKS BEFORE PENTECOST
Holy Spirit, teach us to serve as Jesus served, sacrificing our lives for others.

THE WEEK BEFORE PENTECOST
Spirit of Truth, let us work out our salvation in fear and trembling.

Conclusion of the Day of Rest

LEADER   We now depart from our day of rest. Tomorrow we return to work even as we anticipate God's overflowing blessing on our lives this week. In returning to our work, we also long for our next day of rest as we long for the final day of rest where we will enjoy a great banquet hosted by Jesus Christ our King.

MEMBER   God will prepare a feast with the best food and the greatest of aged wines.

LEADER   What do you think the great banquet will look like? What do you think we will eat? What will the music be like?
The participants imagine the great banquet.
A participant lights the incense and wafts it through the room.

LEADER   We praise you, God, King of the Universe, for you have given us our memories, our desires, and our senses. With great joy we remember the sweetness of this day of rest and anticipate the day of rest to come.

Blessing of the Week

LEADER   May the grace of Christ our Savior, the love of God our Father, and the fellowship of the Spirit be with us throughout this week and forever-more. *Amen.*

The Lighting of the Candle

The leader prays as a participant lights the candle.[39]

LEADER Let us pray. Loving Redeemer, through your passion, reveal to us the truth of the gospel, of self-sacrificing love. Teach us to walk by the light of Christ and submit to your Holy Spirit during this Lenten season.

Meditation or Silence ✠

After a moment of silence or a physical expression of prayer, the leader continues.[40]

LEADER Through your Spirit we are brought to life.

Psalm

ASH WEDNESDAY • Psalm 38:1–5

THURSDAY • Psalm 38:17–22   **FRIDAY** • Psalm 51:1–2

Song for the Season ✠

Sing a song of your choice.

Short Verse

READER Jesus was resolute in his path to the cross: "When the days drew near for him to be taken up, he set his face to go to Jerusalem." Luke 9:51

Short Prayer

READER Kindle in my heart, O God, the flame of love that never ceases.

Scripture Reading

EVERYONE Father, open our eyes that we might see the wonders of your truth.

ASH WEDNESDAY

Jesus said: "Beware of practicing your righteousness before other people in order to be seen by them, for then you will have no reward from your Father who is in heaven." Matthew 6:1–2

Additional Reading: Matthew 6:1–6

Note: The leader may also provide a stone to each family member to remind the family of Jesus' resolve to follow the Father's plan to the cross.

98

THURSDAY

Jesus said: "Very truly I tell you, the Son can do nothing by himself; he can do only what he sees his Father doing, because whatever the Father does the Son also does." John 5:19 (NIV)

Additional Reading: John 15:19–29

FRIDAY

The Torah recounts: "God heard [the groaning of his people] and he remembered his covenant with Abraham, with Isaac, and with Jacob." Exodus 2:24

Additional Reading: Exodus 3:1–22

Open Intercession or Daily Intercession

For daily intercessions see Appendix F.

Prayer for the Week

Almighty God, whose Son was led by the Spirit to be tempted of Satan, help your servants when we are assaulted by many temptations; and, as you know our weaknesses, let each one of us find you mighty to save; through Jesus Christ your Son, our Lord, who lives and reigns with you, one God, now and forever. *Amen.*

—*Based on a collect of the* Book of Common Prayer, *1979*

Song for the Season ✝

Sing a song of your choice.

SECOND WEEK OF LENT

The Lighting of the Candle

The leader prays as a participant lights the candle.

LEADER   Let us pray. Loving Redeemer, through your passion, reveal to us the truth of the gospel, of self-sacrificing love. Teach us to walk by the light of Christ and submit to your Holy Spirit during this season.

Meditation or Silence ✝

After a moment of silence or a physical expression of prayer, the leader continues.

LEADER   Holy Spirit, you purify our hearts.

Psalm

MONDAY • Psalm 102:3–11   **TUESDAY** • Psalm 143:1–2   **WEDNESDAY** • Psalm 6:1–5
THURSDAY • Psalm 143:7–8   **FRIDAY** • Psalm 102:18–22

Song for the Season ✚

Sing a song of your choice.

Short Verse

READER   And Jesus said to everyone, "If anyone would come after me, let him deny himself and take up his cross daily and follow me." Luke 9:23

Short Prayer

READER   Lord, Jesus Christ, fill me, I pray, with your light and life.[41]

Scripture Reading

EVERYONE   Father, open our eyes that we might see the wonders of your truth.

MONDAY

God brought Moses out of the wilderness. Moses performed signs and the people of God believed. Moses' ministry anticipated the coming Messiah, who would also perform the miraculous so that God's people might believe. "Aaron spoke all the words that the LORD has spoken to Moses and did the signs in the sight of the people. And the people believed." Exodus 4:30–31

Additional Reading: Exodus 4:27–31

TUESDAY

As with all kinds of bondage, leaving Egypt was not easy. Pharaoh resisted, making it difficult for God's people to leave. The people blamed Moses for tightening Pharaoh's trip: "The LORD look on you and judge, because you have made us stink in the sight of Pharaoh." Exodus 5:21

Additional Reading: Exodus 5:1–23

WEDNESDAY

The Lord said to Moses, "Now you will see what I will do to Pharaoh: Because of my mighty hand he will let them go." Exodus 6:1 (NIV)

Additional Reading: Exodus 6:1–13

THURSDAY

Though Pharaoh hardened his heart, God would not relent. He told the people: "I will take you to be my people, and I will be your God." Exodus 6:7

Additional Reading: Exodus 7:1–25

100

FRIDAY

Rather than receiving God's mercy, Pharaoh took advantage of the opportunity to renege on his promise. God responded and said: "You may tell in the hearing of your son and of your grandson how I have dealt harshly with the Egyptians and what signs I have done among them, that you may know that I am the LORD." Exodus 10:2

Additional Reading: Exodus 8:1–15

Open Intercession or Daily Intercession

For daily intercessions see Appendix F.

Prayer for the Week

Father in Heaven, by the light of your truth you give sight to the darkness of our sinful eyes. May this season of repentance bring us the blessing of your forgiveness and the gift of your light. Grant this through Christ our Lord. *Amen.*

—*Based on a prayer of the International Committee on English in the Liturgy*

Song for the Season

Sing a song of your choice.

THIRD WEEK OF LENT

The Lighting of the Candle

The leader prays as a participant lights the candle.

LEADER   Let us pray. Loving Redeemer, through your passion, reveal to us the truth of the gospel, of self-sacrificing love. Teach us to walk by the light of Christ and submit to your Holy Spirit during this season.

Meditation or Silence

After a moment of silence or a physical expression of prayer, the leader continues.

LEADER   In your wisdom, we see you all around us.

Psalm

MONDAY • Psalm 32:1–11 TUESDAY • Psalm 38:1–4 WEDNESDAY • Psalm 51:3–6
THURSDAY • Psalm 130:1–4 FRIDAY • Psalm 86:1–7

Song for the Season

Sing a song of your choice.

Short Verse

READER King David wrote: "Search me, O God, and know my heart! Try me and know my thoughts!" Psalm 139:23

Short Prayer

READER O gracious and holy Father, give us wisdom to perceive you.

Scripture Reading

EVERYONE Father, open our eyes that we might see the wonders of your truth.

MONDAY

The power of the Egyptians failed and even the Egyptians knew that God was at work: "Then the magicians said to Pharaoh, 'This is the finger of God.'" Exodus 8:19

Additional Reading: Exodus 8:16–19

TUESDAY

The plagues came upon the Egyptians and Pharaoh asked for God's mercy. But when God relented, Pharaoh hardened his heart. But God said: I do these things "That you may know that I am the LORD in the midst of the earth." Exodus 8:22 (NIV)

Additional Reading: Exodus 8:20–32

WEDNESDAY

Even the Egyptian economy began to suffer, but Pharaoh refused to yield. But God protected his people: "Nothing of all that belongs to the people of Israel shall die." Exodus 9:4

Additional Reading: Exodus 9:1–7

THURSDAY

The health of the people and the animals began to suffer, but Pharaoh refused to yield. Though Egypt was crumbling at the hands of God, still Pharaoh hardened his heart: "He did not listen to them, as the LORD had spoken to Moses." Exodus 9:12

Additional Reading: Exodus 9:8–12

FRIDAY

Shelter proved insufficient as the hail brought Egyptian life to a halt. Even the Egyptians began to revere God, and it was just as God said: "For this purpose I have raised you up, to show you my power, so that my name may be proclaimed in all the earth." Exodus 9:16

Additional Reading: Exodus 9:13–35

Open Intercession or Daily Intercession
For daily intercessions see Appendix F.

Prayer for the Week

O Lord and Master of my life, give me not the spirit of laziness, despair, lust of power, and idle talk. But give me the spirit of sobriety, humility, patience, and love. Yes, O Lord and King, grant me to see my own sins and not to judge my brother. Blessed are you now and for all ages. *Amen.* —*Based on a prayer of St. Ephraim the Syrian*

Song for the Season
Sing a song of your choice.

FOURTH WEEK OF LENT

The Lighting of the Candle
The leader prays as a participant lights the candle.

LEADER   Let us pray. Loving Redeemer, through your passion, reveal to us the truth of the gospel, of self-sacrificing love. Teach us to walk by the light of Christ and submit to your Holy Spirit during this season.

Meditation or Silence
After a moment of silence or a physical expression of prayer, the leader continues.

LEADER   Father, you are our portion. All we need is you.

Psalm

MONDAY • Psalm 95:7–11   TUESDAY • Psalm 31:1–5   WEDNESDAY • Psalm 51:1–4
THURSDAY • Psalm 50:1–6   FRIDAY • Psalm 2:10–12

Song for the Season
Sing a song of your choice.

Short Verse

READER   "Man shall not live by bread alone, but by every word that comes from the mouth of God." Matthew 4:4

Short Prayer

READER O gracious and holy Father, give us intelligence to understand you.

Scripture Reading

EVERYONE Father, open our eyes that we might see the wonders of your truth.

MONDAY

Pharaoh said to Moses: "I have sinned against the LORD your God, and against you."
In turn, God brought relief, but Pharaoh's heart hardened once again. Exodus 10:16

Additional Reading: Exodus 10:1–20

TUESDAY

The sky was covered in darkness. Now, even light had been taken from the Egyptians:
"They did not see one another, nor did anyone rise from his place for three days,
but all the people of Israel had light where they lived." Exodus 10:23

Additional Reading: Exodus 10:21–28

WEDNESDAY

The end was nearing, yet Pharaoh did not submit to God: "'Get away from me;
take care never to see my face again, for on the day you see my face you shall
die.' Moses said, 'As you say! I will not see your face again.'" Exodus 10:28–29

Additional Reading: Exodus 11:1–10

THURSDAY

The blood of the Lamb would save the people of God: "The blood shall be a sign
for you, on the houses where you are. And when I see the blood, I will pass over
you, and no plague will befall you to destroy you, when I strike the land of Egypt."
Exodus 12:13

Additional Reading: Exodus 12:1–28

FRIDAY

God and his people keep the vigil and the feast: "It was a night of watching by
the LORD, to bring them out of the land of Egypt; so this same night is a night of
watching kept to the LORD by all the people of Israel throughout their generations."
Exodus 12:42

Additional Reading: Exodus 12:29–36

Open Intercession or Daily Intercession

For daily intercessions see Appendix F.

Prayer for the Week

Almighty and everlasting God, who willed that our Savior should take upon him our flesh and suffer death upon the cross, that all mankind should follow the example of his great humility, mercifully grant that I may both follow the example of his patience and also partake of his resurrection. *Amen.* —*Based on a prayer of the Short Breviary*

Song for the Season

Sing a song of your choice.

FIFTH WEEK OF LENT

The Lighting of the Candle

The leader prays as a participant lights the candle.

LEADER   Let us pray. Loving Redeemer, through your passion, reveal to us the truth of the gospel, of self-sacrificing love. Teach us to walk by the light of Christ and submit to your Holy Spirit during this season.

Meditation or Silence

After a moment of silence or a physical expression of prayer, the leader continues.

LEADER   Father, we choose to seek you with all our hearts.

Psalm

MONDAY • Psalm 38:9–10   **TUESDAY** • Psalm 131:1–3 **WEDNESDAY** • Psalm 17:6–7
THURSDAY • Psalm 90:1–6   **FRIDAY** • Psalm 144:3–5

Song for the Season

Sing a song of your choice.

Short Verse

READER   "The sacrifices of God are a broken spirit; a broken and contrite heart, O God, you will not despise." Psalm 51:17

Short Prayer

READER   O gracious and holy Father, give us diligence to seek you.

Scripture Reading

EVERYONE   Father, open our eyes that we might see the wonders of your truth.

MONDAY

Moses told the people: "Commemorate this day, the day you came out of Egypt, out of the land of slavery, because the LORD brought you out of it with a mighty hand." Exodus 13:3 (NIV)

Additional Reading: Exodus 13:3–10

TUESDAY

God's presence never left his people: "The LORD went before them by day in a pillar of cloud to lead them along the way, and by night in a pillar of fire to give them light." Exodus 13:21

Additional Reading: Exodus 13:17–22

WEDNESDAY

God demonstrated his faithfulness and his power: "Israel saw the great power that the LORD used against the Egyptians, so the people feared the LORD, and they believed in the LORD and in his servant Moses." Exodus 14:31

Additional Reading: Exodus 14:1–31

THURSDAY

Moses praised God. A song was written that all generations of believers would sing: "You will bring them in and plant them on your own mountain, the place, O LORD, which you have made for your abode, the sanctuary, O Lord, which your hands have established. The LORD will reign forever and ever." Exodus 15:17–18

Additional Reading: Exodus 15:1–21

FRIDAY

Christ, the Passover sacrifice, reconciled the people to God, once for all: "For Christ, our Passover lamb, has been sacrificed. Let us therefore celebrate the festival, not with the old leaven, the leaven of malice and evil, but with the unleavened bread of sincerity and truth." 1 Corinthians 5:7–8

Additional Reading: 1 Corinthians 5:4–8

Open Intercession or Daily Intercession

For daily intercessions see Appendix F

Prayer for the Week

O my all-merciful God and Lord, Jesus Christ, full of mercy: Through your great love you came down and became incarnate in order to save everyone. O Savior, I ask you to continually save me by your grace. If you save anyone because of their works, that would not be grace but only reward of duty, but you are compassionate and full of mercy. I promise that I will work to do your will, my Lord and God, Jesus Christ, all the days of my life and forevermore. *Amen. —Based on a prayer of St. John Chrysostom*

Song for the Season ✠
Sing a song of your choice.

PALM SUNDAY

The Lighting of the Seven Candles ✠
A family member lights the seven candles and then extinguishes one.
Six continue to burn.

LEADER   The light shines in darkness, but the darkness did not understand. He was in the world, and though the world was made through him, the world did not recognize him.

The Symbol of the Palm Branch
The family lays out palm branches for all to see.

READER   As Jesus entered Jerusalem, a very large crowd spread their cloaks on the road, while others cut branches from the trees and spread them on the road. The crowd shouted, "Blessed is he who comes in the name of the Lord. Hosanna in the highest."

Reading
Zechariah 9:9–10; Matthew 21:1–11

LEADER   The palm is a symbol of victory. The people welcomed the one they thought would overthrow the government and establish a new reign. Jesus was moving toward establishing his kingdom, but that kingdom was quite different from the one the people expected.

Prayer for Palm Sunday

LEADER   Jesus, you are the mighty King;
Our palms around you wave;
We throw our garments upon your path
To you who have come to save.
And when you mount your kingly throne,
Through your cross the battle won,

We worship you, O King of heaven,

God's One Eternal Son.

—From the Palm Sunday hymn of the Russian Church

Song for the Season
Sing a song of your choice.

The Lighting of the Seven Candles
A family member lights the seven candles and then extinguishes two.
Five continue to burn.

LEADER The light shines in darkness, but the darkness did not understand. He was in the world, and though the world was made through him, the world did not recognize him.

The Symbol of the Serpent
The leader reminds or shows everyone an image of a brazen serpent or a T-shaped cross.

READER Just as Moses lifted up the snake in the desert, so the Son of Man must be lifted up, that everyone who believes in him may have eternal life.

Reading
Numbers 21:4–9; John 3:14–16

LEADER The image of the lamb is an easier symbol to relate to Jesus and his sacrifice than a serpent. The lamb is innocent, while the serpent is repulsive and dangerous. Though Jesus was the innocent Lamb of God, he who knew no sin became sin that we might be God's righteousness.

Concluding Poem for Monday

LEADER So did the Hebrew prophet raise

The brazen serpent high,

The wounded felt immediate ease,

The camp forbore to die.

"Look upward in the dying hour,

And live," the prophet cries;

But Christ performs a nobler cure,

When Faith lifts up her eyes.

—From "Looking to Jesus," by Isaac Watts

Song for the Season
Sing a song of your choice.

The Lighting of the Seven Candles ✠
A family member lights the seven candles and then extinguishes three.
Four continue to burn.

LEADER The light shines in darkness, but the darkness did not understand. He was in the world, and though the world was made through him, the world did not recognize him.

The Symbol of the Gavel
The leader shows everyone a gavel. (The leader may use an image, if necessary.)

READER Even though Pilate and Herod found Jesus innocent, the people kept shouting, "Crucify him!"

Reading
Luke 22:63–71; Luke 23:1–7; Luke 23:8–12

LEADER Neither Pilate nor Herod found any fault with Jesus. It was not their decision to crucify him. Ironically, it was the very people for whom he sacrificed himself who called for his death. The gavel is an image of Christ's condemnation. Though he was innocent, he took upon himself God's judgment for us.

Concluding Poem for Tuesday

LEADER Worthy is he that once was slain,
The Prince of Peace that groaned and died;
Worthy to rise, and live, and reign
At his Almighty Father's side.
Power and dominion are his due
Who stood condemned at Pilate's bar;
Wisdom belongs to Jesus too,
Though he was charged with madness here.
—*From "Christ's Humiliation and Exaltation," by Isaac Watts*

Song for the Season ✠
Sing a song of your choice.

The Lighting of the Seven Candles ☦

A family member lights the seven candles and then extinguishes four.
Three continue to burn.

LEADER The light shines in darkness, but the darkness did not understand. He was in the world, and though the world was made through him, the world did not recognize him.

The Symbol of the Silver Coins

The leader passes around a bag of coins.

READER This is the night that Jesus was betrayed. One of the twelve disciples—Judas Iscariot—went to the chief priests and asked, "What are you willing to give me if I hand him over to you?" So they gave him thirty silver coins. From then on Judas watched for an opportunity to betray Jesus and hand him over to be arrested.

Reading

Matthew 26:14–25

LEADER Judas is often depicted as the dark, menacing man. However, Judas was trusted with the finances of the disciples and was among Jesus' most intimate friends. No, being betrayed by Judas was like being betrayed by a close friend—one whom you trust and love deeply.

Concluding Poem for Wednesday

LEADER As the sinful woman was bringing her offering of myrrh,
The evil disciple was scheming with lawless men.
She rejoiced in pouring out her precious gift,
While he hastened to sell the Precious One.
She recognized the master,
But Judas parted from him.
She was set free,
But Judas was enslaved.
How terrible is his greed!
How great her repentance!
Savior, you suffered for our sakes.
Grant us also repentance, and save us.
—Based on the matins of the Eastern Orthodox Lenten Triodion

110

Song for the Season
Sing a song of your choice.

The Lighting of the Seven Candles
A family member lights the seven candles and then extinguishes five.
Two continue to burn.

LEADER   The light shines in darkness, but the darkness did not understand. He was in the world, and though the world was made through him, the world did not recognize him.

The Symbol of the Basin and Towel
Before the liturgy, the leader prepares a basin and towel.

LEADER   A new command I give you: love one another. As I have loved you, so you must love one another. By this all men will know that you are my disciples, if you love one another.

Reading
John 13:1–38
Optional: If the leader feels comfortable doing so, he/she may wash the feet of his/her family.

Reading
Matthew 26:31–56

LEADER   Almighty God, you have gathered us in this room, as you gathered your disciples. Teach us to love one another as you love us.

Concluding Prayer for Thursday

LEADER   Almighty Father, whose Son Jesus Christ taught us that what we do for the least of our brothers and sisters, we do also for him; give us the will to be the servant of others as he was the servant of all, who gave up his life and died for us, yet is alive and reigns with you and the Holy Spirit, one God, now and forever. *Amen.*
                    —Based on a traditional collect of the Anglican Church

Song for the Season
Sing a song of your choice.

Spring Home Gathering—The Celebration of Redemption

The family or home group may host or attend The Celebration of Redemption *after this liturgy. See the liturgy for this home gathering on page 129.*

See the liturgy for this home gathering on page 129.

HOLY WEEK—GOOD FRIDAY

The Lighting of the Seven Candles ✠

A family member lights the seven candles and then extinguishes six.
One continues to burn.

LEADER The light shines in darkness, but the darkness did not understand. He was in the world, and though the world was made through him, the world did not recognize him.

The Symbol of the Crown of Thorns or the Nail

Before the liturgy, the leader places a crown of thorns or a nail for all to see.

READER Even though Jesus was innocent, the people asked for Jesus to be crucified. They beat him, spit on him, and humiliated him. They took him away to be crucified.

Reading

Matthew 27:11–56

LEADER But he was pierced through for our transgressions, he was crushed for our iniquities; the chastening for our well-being fell upon him, and by his scourging we are healed. All of us like sheep have gone astray, each of us has turned to his own way; but the LORD has caused the iniquity of us all to fall on him. —*Based on Isaiah 53:5–8a (NASB)*

Concluding Prayer for Good Friday

LEADER Almighty and eternal God, you have restored us to life by the triumphant death and resurrection of Christ. Continue this healing work within us. May we who participate in this mystery never cease to serve you. We ask this in the name of Jesus the Lord. *Amen.*
—*Based on a traditional collect of the Anglican Church*

Song for the Season ✠

Sing a song of your choice.

The Lighting of the Seven Candles ✚

A family member lights the seven candles and then extinguishes them all.
The family pauses and sits in darkness for a few seconds.

LEADER   The light shines in darkness, but the darkness did not understand. He was in the world, and though the world was made through him, the world did not recognize him.

The Symbol of Darkness or Ashes

The participants sit in darkness and may wear black or may reincorporate ashes, which began the season. If ashes are used, the leader may reapply a cross on the forehead of each participant.

LEADER   Tonight we mourn the death of our Lord. All of his followers have scattered. Peter has denied his Lord. All who believe in Jesus are in a state of complete despair.

Reading

Matthew 27:57–66

LEADER   Father, the crucified body of your Son was laid in the tomb. With heavy hearts we remember the consequence of our rebellion and his great sacrifice so that we might live.

Concluding Poem

READER   He who holds the earth in the hollow of his hand has been put to death.
He is held by the earth, to save the dead from hell's grasping hand.
In the tomb they laid you, Christ the Life.
The One who gave me life and breath is now
Lifeless. Breathless.
Carried to the tomb and buried by Joseph's hands.
Now is God's flesh hidden beneath a veil of earth,
In the earth's dark bosom a grain of wheat is laid.
—*Based on the matins of the Eastern Orthodox Lenten Triodion*

Silence

The family observes a few minutes of silence.
When appropriate, the leader may silently and discreetly end this time by walking away. The family does not celebrate the opening of Sabbath on this night and remains in silence for the remainder of the evening. The family may either retire or attend an Easter Vigil later that night to break the silence.

The family can wear either white or new springtime clothes purchased for this season.

The Lighting of the Resurrection Candle ✠

The leader lights a white pillar candle with a white cloth at the base.

LEADER Father, today we celebrate with complete joy the resurrection of your Son, our Lord, Jesus Christ, who is the Light of the World.

READER Enjoy the day of resurrection! Let us be illumined for the great feast! The Passover of the Lord has come and he has passed from death into life. Christ our God now leads us from earth to heaven. We sing the song of victory—Christ is risen from the dead!

—Based on the First Ode of the Easter Canon by St. John of Damascus

The Greeting

LEADER He is risen!

EVERYONE He is risen, indeed!

LEADER He is risen!

EVERYONE Alleluia!

Reading—The Resurrection

John 20:1–21:14

LEADER Father, by raising your Son, Jesus Christ, you conquered death and made new life possible. Today we celebrate his resurrection. Renew us by the Spirit that lives within us.

Song for the Season ✠

Sing a song of your choice.

The Golden Cross

Before the liturgy, the leader places a golden cross for all to see.

LEADER Jesus is not in the grave. He is risen. Jesus came that we might have life and have it abundantly. We are no longer slaves, but we are free. We are free to live as God intended, dwelling in his presence, walking with him. For the same power that raised Jesus from the grave lives in us. May the Spirit of the risen Christ reach into the deepest parts of our souls that we might live the divine life for which he has created us.

114

READER   See the risen Lord of life: To all life he extends his grace. Let all creation rejoice.

The leader makes a sign of the cross over the golden cross.

Song for the Season ✚
Sing a song of your choice, preferably an Alleluia.

Special Activities for Easter Sunday

Easter Morning Breakfast ✚
After the morning home liturgy, the family or home group may host breakfast or brunch.

Worship or Mass and a Community Picnic
After breakfast, the family may attend a worship service or Mass. In the afternoon, the family may fly kites, a symbol of Christ's rising and a symbol of the Holy Spirit to come, and may have a community picnic.

Hiding and finding Easter eggs is also traditional, and in this context the egg represents the Resurrection, the giving of new life.

The Lighting of the Candle

The leader prays as a participant lights the candle.[42]

LEADER   Let us pray. Spirit of the risen Christ, giver of life and light, let the radiance of your presence illumine our home.

Meditation or Silence ✚

After a moment of silence or a physical expression of prayer, the leader continues.

LEADER   Powerful Spirit, you have given us new life.

Psalm

MONDAY • Psalm 113   **TUESDAY** • Psalm 114   **WEDNESDAY** • Psalm 115
THURSDAY • Psalm 116   **FRIDAY** • Psalm 117 or 118

Song for the Season ✚

Sing a song of your choice.

Short Verse

READER   Paul wrote: "If the Spirit of him who raised Jesus from the dead dwells in you, he who raised Christ Jesus from the dead will also give life to your mortal bodies through his Spirit who dwells in you." Romans 8:11

Short Prayer

READER   Risen Christ, make us the living reality of God's presence.

Scripture Reading

EVERYONE   Father, open our eyes that we might see the wonders of your truth.

MONDAY

Isaiah prophesied: "The Spirit of the LORD shall rest upon him, the Spirit of wisdom and of understanding, the Spirit of counsel and of might, the Spirit of knowledge and of the fear of the LORD." Isaiah 11:2

Additional Reading: Isaiah 11

TUESDAY

The Son humbled himself, but the Father exalted him: "God exalted him to the highest place and gave him the name that is above every name." Philippians 2:9 (NIV)

Additional Reading: Philippians 2:5–11

WEDNESDAY

Jesus has fulfilled all the Scriptures: "Beginning with Moses and all the Prophets, [Jesus] explained to them what was said in all the Scriptures concerning himself." Luke 24:27

Additional Reading: Luke 24:13–35

THURSDAY

Jesus' ministry began and ended with him speaking about the kingdom of God: "He presented himself alive to them after his suffering by many proofs, appearing to them during forty days and speaking about the kingdom of God." Acts 1:3

Additional Reading: Acts 1:1–11

FRIDAY

When Jesus ascended, the Holy Spirit rested upon the believers and the church was created: "He led captives in his train and gave gifts to men." Ephesians 4:8 (NIV)

Additional Reading: Ephesians 4:4–24

Open Intercession or Daily Intercession

For daily intercessions see Appendix F

Prayer for the Week

Our God and God of our fathers, give us and all your people your peace, goodness, blessing, life, graciousness, kindness, and mercy. Our Father, cause your divine light to shine upon every member of our family, for it is by your light, O Lord our God, that you have revealed to us the mysteries of your gospel, which sustains life and teaches us the love of kindness, righteousness, blessing, mercy, life, and peace. May it please you to bless this family, this community, this city, and your people everywhere with your peace in every season, yes, even in every hour. We praise you, our Father, for you have made us a people of peace, reconciliation, and redemption. Risen King, reign forever! *Amen.* —*Based on an excerpt from the Jewish Amidah*

Song for the Season ✚

Sing a song of your choice.

Prayer for the Week of the Resurrection

We praise you, O Lord our God, and God of our fathers, God of Abraham, God of Isaac, God of Jacob, God of the Great Cloud of Witnesses, God of the Saints. You are great and mighty, revered and exalted. You generously give us your grace and hold dominion over all things. You remember the faith of our ancestors because you are faithful. You have given us our Redeemer, Jesus Christ. You have given us new life and kept your promise to us, their grandchildren of the faith.

Great King, arise and establish your reign over us. We wait for you. We look forward to the day when your kingdom is completely established. Cause your presence to dwell among us forever, and all our generations will tell of your greatness. Therefore, from this family, may your praise never cease to come from our lips. For you are a great and holy God and a benevolent King. You have conquered death and you are the risen King. Reign forever!

—Adapted from an excerpt from the Jewish Amidah

 SIX WEEKS BEFORE PENTECOST—WEEK OF WISDOM

The Lighting of the Candle
The leader prays as a participant lights the candle.[43]

LEADER   Let us pray. Spirit of the risen Christ, giver of life and light, let the radiance of your presence illumine our home.

Meditation or Silence ✝

After a moment of silence or a physical expression of prayer, the leader continues.

LEADER   Holy Spirit, illumine our minds and give us your understanding.

Psalm

MONDAY • Psalm 119:1–8   TUESDAY • Psalm 119:9–16   WEDNESDAY • Psalm 119:17–24
THURSDAY • Psalm 119:25–32   FRIDAY • Psalm 119:33–40

Song for the Season ✝
Sing a song of your choice.

Short Verse

READER   At the great festival, Jesus announced: "Whoever believes in me, as the Scripture has said, 'Out of his heart will flow rivers of living water.'" John 7:38

Short Prayer

READER   Spirit of truth, set me apart and renew my mind.

Scripture Reading

EVERYONE   Father, open our eyes that we might see the wonders of your truth.

MONDAY

We call out for wisdom and cry aloud for understanding: "Then you will understand the fear of the LORD and find the knowledge of God." Proverbs 2:5 (NIV)

Additional Reading: Proverbs 2:1–10

TUESDAY

"The wind blows wherever it pleases. You hear its sound, but you cannot tell where it comes from or where it is going. So it is with everyone born of the Spirit." John 3:8 (NIV)

Additional Reading: John 3:1–8

WEDNESDAY

And with that he breathed on them and said, "Receive the Holy Spirit. If you forgive anyone his sins, they are forgiven." John 20:22–23 (NIV)

Additional Reading: John 20:19–23

THURSDAY

Jesus said that "when the Spirit of truth comes, he will guide you into all the truth." John 16:13

Additional Reading: John 16:5–15

FRIDAY

The Holy Spirit's presence in Jerusalem fulfilled Joel's prophecy: "I will pour out my Spirit on all people. Your sons and daughters will prophesy, your old men will dream dreams, your young men will see visions. Even on my servants, both men and women, I will pour out my Spirit in those days." Joel 2:28–29 (NIV)

Additional Reading: Joel 2:12–29

Open Intercession or Daily Intercession

For daily intercessions see Appendix F.

Prayer for the Week

O Lord Jesus Christ, who before ascending into heaven promised to send the Holy Spirit to finish your work in the souls of your apostles and disciples, grant us that the same Holy Spirit might perfect our souls by the work of your grace and your love.

Grant us the *Spirit of Wisdom* to enlighten our minds with the light of your divine truth. Make us, dear Lord, your true disciples, and give us life in all things with your Spirit. Amen. —*Based on the novena to the Seven Gifts of the Holy Spirit*

Song for the Season ✟
Sing a song of your choice.

The Lighting of the Candle
The leader prays as a participant lights the candle.
LEADER Let us pray. Spirit of the risen Christ, giver of life and light, let the radiance of your presence illumine our home.

Meditation or Silence ✟
After a moment of silence or a physical expression of prayer, the leader continues.
LEADER Holy Spirit, you guide us and counsel us in the way of peace.

Psalm
MONDAY • Psalm 119:41–48 TUESDAY • Psalm 119:49–56 WEDNESDAY • Psalm 119:57–64
THURSDAY • Psalm 119:65–72 FRIDAY • Psalm 119:73–80

Song for the Season ✟
Sing a song of your choice.

Short Verse
READER Jesus told Nicodemus: "The wind blows where it wishes, and you hear its sound, but you do not know where it comes from or where it goes. So it is with everyone who is born of the Spirit." John 3:8

Short Prayer
READER Holy Spirit, awaken us from indifference. Give us active understanding.

Scripture Reading
EVERYONE Father, open our eyes that we might see the wonders of your truth.

MONDAY
God promised: "I will put my Spirit within you, and you shall live." Ezekiel 37:14
Additional Reading: Ezekiel 37:11–14

TUESDAY

God declared: "I will put my law within them, and I will write it on their hearts. And I will be their God, and they shall be my people." Jeremiah 31:33

Additional Reading: Jeremiah 31

WEDNESDAY

Jesus said it was to our advantage that he return to the Father. Upon his departure he promised that the Counselor would come: "When the Spirit of truth comes, he will guide you into all the truth." John 16:13

Additional Reading: John 16:5-15

THURSDAY

Our minds are limited and our words are weak, but we have a Helper: "The Spirit himself intercedes for us with groanings too deep for words." Romans 8:26

Additional Reading: Romans 8:26–27

FRIDAY

Jesus said: "The Helper, the Holy Spirit, whom the Father will send in my name, he will teach you all things and bring to remembrance all that I have said to you." John 14:26

Additional Reading: John 14:15–26

Open Intercession or Daily Intercession
For daily intercessions see Appendix F.

Prayer for the Week

O Lord Jesus Christ, who before ascending into heaven promised to send the Holy Spirit to finish your work in the souls of your apostles and disciples, grant us that the same Holy Spirit might perfect our souls by the work of your grace and your love.

Grant us the *Spirit of Counsel,* that we may ever choose the surest way of pleasing God. Make us, dear Lord, your true disciples, and give us life in all things with your Spirit. Amen. —*Based on the Novena to the Seven Gifts of the Holy Spirit*

Song for the Season ✠
Sing a song of your choice.

The Lighting of the Candle

The leader prays as a participant lights the candle.

LEADER   Let us pray. Spirit of the risen Christ, giver of life and light, let the radiance of your presence illumine our home.

Meditation or Silence ✚

After a moment of silence or a physical expression of prayer, the leader continues.

LEADER   Holy Spirit, you give us strength for every day.

Psalm

MONDAY • Psalm 119:81–88   TUESDAY • Psalm 119:89–96   WEDNESDAY • Psalm 119:97–104
THURSDAY • Psalm 119:105–112   FRIDAY • Psalm 119:113–120

Song for the Season ✚

Sing a song of your choice.

Short Verse

READER   Jesus told his disciples: "You will receive power when the Holy Spirit has come upon you, and you will be my witnesses in Jerusalem and in all Judea and Samaria, and to the end of the earth." Acts 1:8

Short Prayer

READER   Good Counselor, indwell the deepest, inmost parts of our souls.

Scripture Reading

EVERYONE   Father, open our eyes that we might see the wonders of your truth.

MONDAY

Babel is the opposite of Pentecost. The world tries to create unity through uniformity. The Spirit creates unity in diversity: "And how is it that we hear, each of us in his own native language?" Acts 2:8

Additional Reading: Genesis 11:1–9; 2:1–13

TUESDAY

God loves for his people to dwell in the oneness of his love: "Behold, how good and pleasant it is when brothers dwell in unity!" Psalm 133:1

Additional Reading: Exodus 29:7; Psalm 133

WEDNESDAY

Jesus would fulfill Isaiah's prophecy: "The Spirit of the LORD God is upon me, because the LORD has anointed me to bring good news to the poor." Isaiah 61:1

Additional Reading: Isaiah 61:1–4; Luke 4:16–21

THURSDAY

The Spirit brought all kinds of people together. God's presence transcends nationality, age, gender, and social class and brings uncommon things into divine unity: "And they were all filled with the Holy Spirit and began to speak in other tongues as the Spirit gave them utterance." Acts 2:4

Additional Reading: Acts 2:1–12

FRIDAY

The Holy Spirit is God's gift of promise: "[He] has also put his seal on us and given us his Spirit in our hearts as a guarantee." 2 Corinthians 1:22

Additional Reading: 2 Corinthians 1:21–22; 1 John 2:27–28

Open Intercession or Daily Intercession
For daily intercessions see Appendix F.

Prayer for the Week

O Lord Jesus Christ, who before ascending into heaven promised to send the Holy Spirit to finish your work in the souls of your apostles and disciples, grant us that the same Holy Spirit might perfect our souls by the work of your grace and your love.

Grant us the *Spirit of Endurance*, that we may bear our cross with you, and that we may overcome with courage all the obstacles that oppose our following you. Make us, dear Lord, your true disciples, and give us life in all things with your Spirit. Amen. —*Based on the novena to the Seven Gifts of the Holy Spirit*

Song for the Season ✠
Sing a song of your choice.

The Lighting of the Candle

The leader prays as a participant lights the candle.

LEADER   Let us pray. Spirit of the risen Christ, giver of life and light, let the radiance of your presence illumine our home.

Meditation or Silence ✦

After a moment of silence or a physical expression of prayer, the leader continues.

LEADER   Holy Spirit, spark in us a renewed sense of creativity and curiosity.

Psalm

MONDAY • Psalm 119:121–128 TUESDAY • Psalm 119:129–136
WEDNESDAY • Psalm 119:137–144
THURSDAY •Psalm 119:145–152 FRIDAY • Psalm 119:153–160

Song for the Season ✦

Sing a song of your choice.

Short Verse

READER   John wrote: "But the anointing that you received from him abides in you, and you have no need that anyone should teach you. But as his anointing teaches you about everything, and is true, and is no lie—just as it has taught you, abide in him." I John 2:27

Short Prayer

READER   Spirit of Truth, give us faith to inquire, explore, and create.

Scripture Reading

EVERYONE   Father, open our eyes that we might see the wonders of your truth.

MONDAY

From the very beginning, God intended for us to dwell with him, to walk with him on holy ground: "Take your sandals off your feet, for the place on which you are standing is holy ground." Exodus 3:5

Additional Reading: Exodus 3:2–6

TUESDAY

When God set them free from Egypt, he stayed close to his people and led them every step of the way: "The LORD your God who goes before you will himself fight for you, just as he did for you in Egypt before your eyes, and in the wilderness, where you have seen how the LORD your God carried you, as a man carries his son." Deuteronomy 1:30–31

Additional Reading: Exodus 13:21–22; Deuteronomy 1:30–33

WEDNESDAY

Nehemiah reminded God's people, more than a thousand years later, that it was God who led them and God who would continue to lead them. Nehemiah prayed: "You are the LORD, you alone. . . . You gave them bread from heaven for their hunger and brought water for them out of the rock for their thirst." Nehemiah 9:6, 15

Additional Reading: Nehemiah 9:12–21

THURSDAY

Jesus prayed for his disciples and for us: "Sanctify them in the truth; your word is truth. As you sent me into the world, so I have sent them into the world." John 17:17–18

Additional Reading: John 17:6–19

FRIDAY

God created us for freedom: "Now the Lord is the Spirit, and where the Spirit of the Lord is, there is freedom." 2 Corinthians 3:17

Additional Reading: 2 Corinthians 3:12–18

Open Intercession or Daily Intercession
For daily intercessions see Appendix F.

Prayer for the Week

O Lord Jesus Christ, who before ascending into heaven promised to send the Holy Spirit to finish your work in the souls of your apostles and disciples, grant us that the same Holy Spirit might perfect our souls by the work of your grace and your love.

Grant us the *Spirit of Inquiry* that we may know you and be set free to explore the world around us. Make us, dear Lord, your true disciples, and give us life in all things with your Spirit. Amen. —*Based on the novena to the Seven Gifts of the Holy Spirit*

Song for the Season
Sing a song of your choice.

The Lighting of the Candle

The leader prays as a participant lights the candle.

LEADER   Let us pray. Spirit of the risen Christ, giver of life and light, let the radiance of your presence illumine our home.

Meditation or Silence ✠

After a moment of silence or a physical expression of prayer, the leader continues.

LEADER   Father, give us humble hearts.

Psalm

MONDAY • Psalm 119:161–168   TUESDAY • Psalm 119:169–176
WEDNESDAY • Psalm 18:25–30   THURSDAY • Psalm 56:1–4   FRIDAY • Psalm 56:8–11

Song for the Season ✠

Sing a song of your choice.

Short Verse

READER   John the Baptist told the crowds: "I baptize you with water for repentance, but he who is coming after me is mightier than I, whose sandals I am not worthy to carry. He will baptize you with the Holy Spirit and fire." Matthew 3:11

Short Prayer

READER   Holy Spirit, teach us to serve as Jesus served, sacrificing our lives for others.

Scripture Reading

EVERYONE   Father, open our eyes that we might see the wonders of your truth.

MONDAY

"The fear of the LORD is the beginning of knowledge." Proverbs 1:7

Additional Reading: Proverbs 1:1–7

TUESDAY

God commanded his people to keep the feast of the first fruits, a sign that we might be his first fruits. Paul reminded us: "God chose you as the firstfruits to be saved, through sanctification by the Spirit and belief in the truth." 2 Thessalonians 2:13

Additional Reading: Leviticus 23:9–21; 2 Thessalonians 2:13–17

WEDNESDAY

One of Jesus' closest disciples reminded us: "Of [God's] own will he brought us forth by the word of truth, that we should be a kind of firstfruits of his creatures." James 1:18

Additional Reading: James 1:17–18

THURSDAY

Everything God has made yearns for redemption: "Not only the creation, but we ourselves, who have the firstfruits of the Spirit, groan inwardly as we wait eagerly for adoption as sons, the redemption of our bodies." Romans 8:23

Additional Reading: Romans 8:18–25

FRIDAY

God gave us his Spirit to live a divine life: "The fruit of the Spirit is love, joy, peace, patience, kindness, goodness, faithfulness, gentleness, self-control." Galatians 5:22–23

Additional Reading: Galatians 5:16–23

Open Intercession or Daily Intercession
For daily intercessions see Appendix F.

Prayer for the Week

O Lord Jesus Christ, who before ascending into heaven promised to send the Holy Spirit to finish your work in the souls of your apostles and disciples, grant us that the same Holy Spirit might perfect our souls by the work of your grace and your love.

Grant us the *Spirit of Service* that we may find the service of God sweet and amiable, and finally, make us, dear Lord, your true disciples, and give us life in all things with your Spirit. Amen. —*Based on the novena to the Seven Gifts of the Holy Spirit*

Song for the Season ✠
Sing a song of your choice.

The Lighting of the Candle

The leader prays as a participant lights the candle.

LEADER   Let us pray. Spirit of the risen Christ, giver of life and light, let the radiance of your presence illumine our home.

Meditation or Silence ✠

After a moment of silence or a physical expression of prayer, the leader continues.

LEADER   Father, your holy presence simultaneously brings humility and integrity.

Psalm

MONDAY • Psalm 78:1–4 TUESDAY • Psalm 106:6–12 WEDNESDAY • Psalm 107:17–21
THURSDAY • Psalm 107:1–9 FRIDAY • Psalm 67:1–7

Song for the Season ✠

Sing a song of your choice.

Short Verse

READER   Jesus said: "I will ask the Father, and he will give you another Helper. . . . You know him, for he dwells with you and will be in you." John 14:16–17

Short Prayer

READER   Spirit of Truth, let us work out our salvation in fear and trembling.

Scripture Reading

EVERYONE   Father, open our eyes that we might see the wonders of your truth.

MONDAY

The climax of the Exodus occurs when God's glory fills the tabernacle—his presence is no longer outside the camp, but in the midst of his people: "The glory of the LORD filled the tabernacle." Exodus 40:35

Additional Reading: Exodus 40:34–38

TUESDAY

Solomon believed that David's promise was fulfilled, but this king of peace and this temple were only a shadow of the King and Temple to come: "Blessed be the LORD, the God of Israel, who with his hand has fulfilled what he promised." I Kings 8:15

Additional Reading: 1 Kings 8:12–27

WEDNESDAY
Ezra and Nehemiah began to rebuild the temple and city. In the fallen city of Jerusalem they said: "Let the house of God be rebuilt on its site." But this rebuilding only anticipated the temple and city that would never be shaken. Ezra 5:15

Additional Reading: Ezra 5:8–13

THURSDAY
Paul asked: "Do you not know that you are God's temple and that God's Spirit dwells in you?" I Corinthians 3:16

Additional Reading: 1 Corinthians 3:10–16

FRIDAY
John saw the great revelation: "I saw no temple in the city, for its temple is the Lord God the Almighty and the Lamb." Revelation 21:22

Additional Reading: Revelation 21:18–26

Open Intercession or Daily Intercession
For daily intercessions see Appendix F.

Prayer for the Week
Lord Jesus Christ, who before ascending into heaven promised to send the Holy Spirit to finish your work in the souls of your apostles and disciples, grant us that the same Holy Spirit might perfect our souls by the work of your grace and your love.

Grant us the *Spirit of Holy Fear* that we may be filled with a loving reverence toward you and may reject anything that displeases you. Make us, dear Lord, your true disciples, and give us life in all things with your Spirit. *Amen. —Based on the novena to the Seven Gifts of the Holy Spirit*

Song for the Season ✠
Sing a song of your choice.

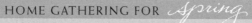

The Celebration of Redemption

The second major home gathering of the year is *The Celebration of Redemption*, which retells the story of the Exodus. Though this is the second home gathering of the liturgical calendar, this is the most ancient and the greatest of all the home celebrations, as it explains the beginning of the story of redemption and our journey to become the people of God. Families and home groups are encouraged to celebrate this gathering on Maundy Thursday.

PREPARING FOR *The Celebration of Redemption*

FOOD AND SYMBOLS ✚ Below is a list of the symbols necessary for this home gathering. This gathering is more involved than the others, but is rich in heritage and meaning.

Symbols:

> Numerous pieces of regular leavened bread
> White pillar candles
> Four special cups for the leader for wine (or grape juice)
> Wine glasses for each participant
> Plenty of wine (or grape juice)
> Pitcher of water
> Basin and white towel
> Stack of three pieces of unleavened bread (matzah) in a cloth napkin
> Dish of salt water (or several dishes if a large group)
> Special plate (the Seder plate) set aside for the following symbols:
>> Parsley
>> Lamb shank bone (or other bone, if lamb bone is unavailable)
>> Hard boiled egg
>> Bitter herbs (horseradish)
>> Mixture of apples, honey, and nuts (called *charoset*)
>> Lamb entrée (or beef, if lamb is unavailable)

BEFORE THE CELEBRATION ✚ Before the celebration begins, the family or home group prepares the house with a thorough cleaning, which helps to create anticipation. The family hides some pieces of leavened bread around the house and sets the table for the meal.

READERS The host may select the readers prior to the meal.

LITURGY FOR

The Celebration of Redemption

LEADER Before we begin our celebration, we must prepare ourselves by getting rid of the leaven in our house. Leaven represents sin. The apostle Paul said a little sin goes a long way, infecting all aspects of our lives, and the lives of those around us.

The leader asks the children to search for the hidden pieces of bread. Next, the pieces of bread may be burned in a small fire or carried outside the home.

LEADER God, you have searched us and you know our thoughts. Cleanse us and remove all sin that is destructive to us and to those we love.

Begin the liturgy before the meal.

The Lighting of the Candles

LEADER Peace be with you.

EVERYONE And also with you.

LEADER Everyone please stand and welcome God's presence for this time of celebration.

Everyone stands around the table as a woman lights the candles.

LEADER We praise you, God, King of the Universe, for you have given us the light of life. May the light of your presence fill our hearts, this time, and this season with joy.

Song for the Season ✠

Sing a song of your choice.

The First Cup—We Are Set Apart

LEADER Please be seated. We begin *The Celebration of Redemption* by saying a blessing over the first cup. This is the Cup of Sanctification, or the cup that sets us apart.

The four cups of wine used in this celebration symbolize the four promises made by God as told in Exodus 6:6–7:

> The First Cup: The Cup of Sanctification
> The Second Cup: The Cup of Deliverance
> The Third Cup: The Cup of Redemption
> The Fourth Cup: The Cup of Restoration

LEADER   We are set apart. God has set us apart to be his people.

The leader pours wine or juice into the first cup.

LEADER   We praise you, God, King of the Universe, who set us apart as your people. This cup reminds us of our rich heritage of faith and our call to freedom. Let us drink the Cup of Sanctification.

The leader drinks from the first cup and all participants drink from their wine glasses.

The Basin and the Towel—We Are Clean

LEADER   God says that we are clean in him. Let us take the basin and wash our hands.

Each person washes his or her hands in the basin and dries them with the towel.

LEADER   Most likely this is the point where Jesus washed the disciples' feet. After the disciples washed their hands, Jesus would have taken the basin and assumed the role of a humble servant. He then began to wash his disciples' feet. Imagine their surprise.

Song for the Season ✠

Sing a song of your choice.

The Green Vegetable—New Life

LEADER   God has given new life. Spring is here and new life is budding all around us.

The leader takes a sprig of fresh parsley and holds it up.

LEADER   This green vegetable represents life, created and sustained by the Lord our God.

MEN   Arise, my love, and come away; for now the winter is past, the rain is over and gone, the flowers appear on the earth, the time of singing has come. Arise, my love, my fair one, and come away.

WOMEN   My beloved is mine and I am his. He brought me to his banquet, and his intention toward me is love.

LEADER   And yet as good as God intends life to be, it is often mixed with tears. Tonight we are not simply celebrating springtime or love. We are celebrating the freedom and deliverance that God brought to us as slaves. Let us never forget that the struggle for freedom begins in suffering, and that life is sometimes immersed in tears.

LEADER   We praise you, God, King of the Universe, for you bring forth fruit from the earth.

Everyone dips a sprig of parsley in the salt water and eats.

The Breaking of the Bread

The leader takes the middle piece of unleavened bread and holds it up.

LEADER This is the bread of affliction that our ancestors ate in the land of Egypt. All who are hungry, come and eat.

The leader breaks the bread in half and places one half back in the cloth. The half of the bread placed back into the cloth is called the afikomen *and will be used later. The half that is unwrapped will be used within this portion of the liturgy.*

LEADER This broken piece of bread is symbolic of Jesus. Like this bread, Jesus was perfect, without any leaven. These holes and blemishes in the bread symbolize that his body was pierced and beaten for our sins, and by his wounds we are healed. Consider, too, the triune God. It is the second piece that is chosen and broken. Then the piece is wrapped up and carefully hidden from view. This is an image of the death, burial, and ultimately the resurrection of Jesus from the dead.

Song for the Season ✠

Sing a song of your choice.

The Story

The leader selects a child or a few children to ask the questions for this portion of the liturgy.

LEADER The story is the heart of the meal and is recounted as a parent telling the Exodus story to his children, following the biblical command, "In time, your children will ask . . . then you shall tell them" (Deuteronomy 6:20–21). The questions are usually asked by the youngest child present who can read well, with the answers given by a father or grandfather.

CHILD Why is this night different from all other nights?

PEOPLE Once we were slaves, but the Lord in his goodness brought us out with a mighty hand and an outstretched arm. We remember that we were enslaved by our sins, but God in his goodness forgave us and called us to be his people.

LEADER We have gathered to remember who God has created us to be and what God has done for us, and to tell our children the story of God's grace and deliverance.

WOMAN God promised Abraham and Sarah that they would be a great people, a promise he renewed to each generation, to Isaac and Jacob. As time passed, Jacob's children came to live in the land of Egypt, where his son Joseph was advisor to Pharaoh. But years passed and another

Pharaoh came to power who did not remember Joseph and did not know God. So, he enslaved the Israelites. He forced them to work hard making bricks of clay and straw to build his cities. As the people increased in numbers, he feared that they might rebel against him, so he ordered every newborn boy drowned. God's people knew only toil, suffering, and tears.

LEADER The people cried out from their oppression. God heard their cry and remembered the covenant he had made with Abraham. Through a wise mother and sister, God saved the life of the boy Moses from the hands of Pharaoh. After Moses had grown up, God sent him to deliver the Israelites from the slavery of Egypt, and promised him that God would be with him.

WOMAN And yet when Moses asked Pharaoh to free the Israelites, Pharaoh refused and increased their labor. So God sent ten plagues on Pharaoh and the land of Egypt so they might know that the Lord is God, and let the people go.

LEADER In a moment we will drink the second cup, the Cup of Deliverance, and we will celebrate God's deliverance of us from slavery. Though we celebrate our salvation, we lament that lives were sacrificed to bring about the release of God's people from the slavery of Egypt. As we recount the plagues, we will spill a drop of wine from our cups for each plague, to recall the cost of sin and the consequences of evil in a fallen world.

As each plague is recited, the leader removes a single drop of wine or juice with his or her finger, and places it on a plate. DO NOT drink from the second cup yet.

LEADER Blood. Frogs. Lice. Swarms. Cattle disease. Boils. Hail. Locusts. Darkness. Death of the firstborn.

The leader replaces the second cup on the table WITHOUT drinking.

WOMAN Even after the plagues, Pharaoh continued to refuse to let the people go until the last plague, the death of the firstborn of all of Egypt, convinced him to release the people. By following God's instructions and putting the blood of a lamb on the doorposts of their houses, the Israelites were spared this plague as death "passed over" their houses.

The leader removes the lamb bone from the Seder plate and holds it up.

LEADER This is the symbol of the Passover lamb, sacrificed so that we might live.

PEOPLE Behold the Lamb of God, who takes away the sin of the world!

LEADER   The death of Jesus, the Lamb of God, has perfectly and eternally satisfied the need for sacrifice for us to become acceptable to God. In his death, we are given new life.

The leader replaces the bone on the Seder plate and removes the egg from the Seder plate.

LEADER   Though Jesus' sacrifice is complete and we are reconciled to God, redemption is still in progress. The roasted egg reminds us that life is still hard and in need of redemption. The egg is a symbol of mourning, the suppression of new life. We lament the absence of God's kingdom where we live: broken families, the greed inherent to our economy, systemic exploitation of the poor, the hunger of the developing world, political corruption, abuse of God's creation, ethical indifference—all are signs that slavery to sin still exists.

The leader replaces the roasted egg on the Seder plate.

WOMAN   As the Israelites were leaving, Pharaoh changed his mind and sent his army after them. Trapped between Pharaoh's army and the Red Sea, the Israelites had nowhere to go. But God told Moses to lift his staff over the sea, and God parted the waters. The Egyptians tried to follow, but the waters closed back over them. When the Israelites saw they were free, they rejoiced and praised God.

PEOPLE: We praise you, God, King of the Universe, for you hear the cries of the oppressed and bring freedom to the captive.

Song for the Season ✝

Sing a song of your choice.

The Bread of Life

CHILD   Why on all other nights do we eat bread with leaven, but tonight we eat unleavened bread?

The leader takes the unwrapped portion of the broken half of unleavened bread and holds it up.

LEADER   Tonight we eat unleavened bread because our ancestors in Egypt had to leave in a hurry and they could not wait for their bread to rise.

The leader takes the top piece, and the unwrapped half of the unleavened bread, and distributes pieces to every participant.

LEADER   We praise you, God, King of the Universe, for you provide our daily bread and meet our every need.

The people eat a small piece of unleavened bread.

Bitterness

CHILD Why on all other nights do we eat all kinds of herbs, but on this night we eat bitter herbs?

The leader takes the horseradish and holds it up.

LEADER Tonight we eat bitter herbs to remember the difficulty of slavery.

PEOPLE As sweet as our lives are now, we must never forget the bitterness of bondage.

Everyone puts a small amount of the bitter herb on his or her plate.

LEADER Let us remember how bitter our slavery was. As we eat, let us allow the bitter taste to bring tears of compassion for those who are still enslaved.

Everyone eats the bitter herb with a small piece of unleavened bread.

Sweetness

CHILD Why on all other nights do we not dip even once, but tonight we dip twice?

The leader takes a sprig of parsley and the charoset *and holds them up.*

LEADER We have already dipped the green vegetable. We will also dip the *charoset*. Tonight we dip twice to remind us of the sweetness that God brings even from bitterness.

PEOPLE How sweet is your word to my taste, sweeter than honey to my mouth!

LEADER As we are reminded of the bitterness of our slavery, so too are we reminded of the hope that we have in our Lord, even when circumstances are difficult.

Everyone puts a small amount of charoset *on his or her plate, while the third piece of unleavened bread is passed around.*

LEADER *Charoset* is a sweet mixture of apples, honey, and nuts. It symbolizes the mixture of clay and straw that the Israelites used to make bricks for Pharaoh's cities. But the sweetness of the mixture also reminds us that even out of the depths of pain and despair, God can bring redemption. We praise you, God, King of the Universe, for you bring redemption from sorrow.

The people eat the charoset *with the unleavened bread.*

The People of God

CHILD   Why on all other nights do we usually eat with only a few people, but on this night we eat with so many people?

LEADER   Tonight we eat with other people whom God has set free. God has called us together to serve and love each other, to celebrate with each other, and also to mourn with each other. He has called us to share our lives, living in the truth of his freedom. In doing so, we indwell God's presence here on earth. We are the people of God.

The Second Cup of Deliverance

The leader takes the second cup, and raises it.

LEADER   With the second cup we celebrate God's deliverance. We praise you, God, King of the Universe, for you have brought us from bondage to freedom, from sorrow to joy, from darkness to light, from slavery to redemption.

The leader drinks from the second cup and all participants drink from their wine glasses.

The people pass the peace while the designated people retrieve the lamb dinner and present it.

The Table

LEADER   It is time to eat. Everyone will now say a blessing over the food.

EVERYONE   We praise you, God, King of the Universe, for you have set us free because of the Passover Lamb, our Lord, our Savior, Jesus Christ.

The leader discreetly takes the middle piece of broken unleavened bread, wrapped in cloth, and hides it for the children to find after dinner. This is the afikomen, *mentioned above.*

[The liturgy pauses during the meal.]

Renewal

LEADER   As we continue in our ceremony, we take a moment to renew our focus.

Everyone passes the basin and towel and washes his or her hands.

The Hidden and the Cup of Redemption

LEADER   The time has come to reveal the hidden.

The children search for the afikomen. *When a child returns the* afikomen *to the leader, all children receive a prize and celebrate. The leader then unwraps the* afikomen. *The leader refills the third cup while the people refill their cups.*

LEADER   Jesus celebrated Passover with his disciples on the night before he was crucified.

The people all take a piece of the broken bread. The leader then holds up a piece.

LEADER   This broken bread of redemption reminds us of the broken body of our Lord Jesus Christ. Take and eat this, remembering that Jesus was broken for our sins.

All eat the bread. When finished, the leader holds up the cup.

LEADER   This cup reminds us of the blood of our Lord Jesus Christ. Drink this, remembering that his blood was poured out so that we might be redeemed.

All drink from the cup.

LEADER   We were in slavery, but God sent his Son so that we might be set free.

PEOPLE   Because of Jesus' sacrifice we are no longer slaves, but sons and daughters. To him who loves us and has freed us from our sins, be glory and power forever and ever!

The Power of the Risen Christ

LEADER   Jesus Christ our Lord is not only our sacrifice and our liberation, but he is also our new life. He came that we might have life and have it abundantly. Therefore, we celebrate his resurrection and the new life that he has given us. He is risen.

PEOPLE   He is risen, indeed!

LEADER   He is risen!

PEOPLE   Hallelujah!

LEADER   We, along with the angels of God, are rejoicing. The tomb is empty. Christ is risen from the dead. Glory and power are his, forever and ever.

The Cup of Restoration and Time of Praise

LEADER   We come to the fourth and final cup, the Cup of Restoration.

PEOPLE   Give thanks to the Lord, for he is good, for his unfailing loves endures forever.

LEADER   When Jesus led the Passover Seder, he told his disciples that he would not drink the fourth cup until he drank with them in the coming kingdom. As Jesus left, he promised he would come again and restore all things.

The leader fills the fourth cup and all raise their wine glasses.

LEADER   We raise our glasses a fourth time in thanksgiving for God's enduring grace and love for us. We praise you, God, King of the Universe, for you have adopted us as your children and allowed us to call you "Father."

Everyone drinks, relaxes, and enjoys a time of praise.

Song for the Season ✠

Sing a song or songs of your choice.

The Fulfillment

LEADER   One day God's kingdom will be established forever. Until then, we pray that his kingdom is present where we live. As God's people we pray:

PEOPLE   Our Father, who art in heaven, hallowed be your name. Your kingdom come, your will be done, on earth as it is in heaven. Give us today our daily bread, and forgive us our sins, as we forgive those who sin against us. Lead us not into temptation, but deliver us from evil. For yours is the kingdom, the power, and the glory forever. *Amen.*

LEADER   The traditional conclusion of this liturgy is a hope for the future expressed by the Jewish people throughout history: "Next year in Jerusalem." We will conclude this meal with the same expression of hope and faith in God, as we await the coming of a new Jerusalem, the fulfillment of God's kingdom and the completion of God's redemptive story.

PEOPLE   Next year in the new Jerusalem, the City of God!

LEADER   Jesus says, "Yes, I am coming soon."

PEOPLE   *Amen.* Come, Lord Jesus.

LEADER   The grace of the Lord Jesus be with God's people everywhere. *Amen.* *The leader extinguishes the Passover candles.*

Summer

Preparing for the Season   141

✠ *This symbol denotes that additional resources or reminders may be found at the athomewithgod.org website.*

Preparing for the Season

Summer is entirely within an ordinary season, which we divide into two parts:

THE TIME OF THE CHURCH—Pentecost through the end of June

THE TIME OF THE KINGDOM—July and August

The Time of the Church

Pentecost celebrates the arrival of the Holy Spirit and the formation of the church, God's new dwelling place. The biblical and redemptive themes focus on God's intent to dwell with his people and incarnate himself within them. The themes of Pentecost may be celebrated from Pentecost Sunday to the end of June. Pentecost falls as early as May 11 and as late as June 12. To compensate for the variable time, intermediary weeks have been included.

The Time of the Kingdom

The first weekend of July always begins the Time of the Kingdom, which is the second portion of the ordinary time of the summer.[44] Stemming from Pentecost, the time focuses upon the expression of the peaceable kingdom of God here on earth. This season lasts from the first weekend in July to the end of August.

Traditions for the Season

SPECIAL ACTIVITIES ✠

SEEDS AND PLANTING Families or home groups may wish to plant a garden together; this is an excellent family or community-building project. The seeds and the growth process are symbols of the kingdom, as Jesus told us that the kingdom of God is like a mustard seed. The kingdom starts small, but grows from a seed into something larger and fruitful.

PICNICS AND MUSIC Families or home groups may enjoy gathering during this season for picnics that include good foods and singing together. The theology of this season hearkens to a time where everything "is as it should be." God's kingdom is a place of abundance and peace. These times are intended to be a taste of the kingdom of God here on earth.

SPECIAL SYMBOLS FOR THE SEASON

Below is a list of signs and symbols that could be used for these seasons.

RED Red is the liturgical color for Pentecost and symbolizes the fire of the Holy Spirit that descended during the birth of the church in Jerusalem.

GREEN Green is the color for the ordinary time and represents new life and growth.

OLIVES Olives, olive branches, olive trees, and olive oil are consistently used throughout Scripture as symbols of blessing and peace.

LEMONADES, LIMEADES, AND SANGRIAS After *The Celebration of Redemption*, we eat and drink lighter, sweeter, and fruitier drinks, symbolizing the sweetness of the divine life, the freedom that we have in Christ and the enjoyment of God and his kingdom.

SUMMER FRUITS AND VEGETABLES Summer fruits and vegetables (especially if they are straight from the garden or from a local farm) are perfect for the season and represent the first fruits of the Spirit and the newness of life in Christ.

HONEY, CHEESECAKES, AND CHEESE PASTRIES In Exodus 3, God's promise to his people is that he will lead them from bondage to a land flowing with milk and honey. These foods are used as a symbol of the land of promise.

HOME GATHERING

THE CELEBRATION OF NEW LIFE Rather than a Sabbath celebration, a home gathering celebration is used on the weekend of Pentecost. The home gathering for this season centers on the biblical themes of Pentecost and, most important, on God's desire to dwell within his people. In turn, this home liturgy is simpler and less involved than the Passover liturgy. It focuses on our joy and freedom in God. No longer is God's presence merely an external expression. God lives within those who believe. Therefore, this home gathering should have a simple, harmonious, and serene mood.

The Lighting of the Candle

LEADER   Come, Holy Spirit, kindle the hearts of the faithful and renew us in the fire of your love.

A participant lights the candle for the season.[45]

MEMBER   We praise you, God, King of the Universe, for you have given us Jesus Christ and his Holy Spirit, our counselor, helper, and advocate.

EVERYONE   We praise you, God, Creator and Redeemer.

LEADER   We praise you, God, King of the Universe, for you have given us this day of rest. Because of Jesus' ascension, your Spirit has come to dwell in us. May the fire of your presence rest on this home and give us joy and peace. *Amen.*

The Blessing

Families with children may want to insert a short prayer for each child here.

LEADER   As the Holy Spirit brought unity to the various believers at Jerusalem, may we experience oneness within the body of Christ. Though we are made of many parts, may we live and act as one.

Song of Blessing ✠

The Lord bless you and keep you;
The Lord make his face shine upon you.
The Lord be gracious to you.
And give you his peace, forever.

Telling the Redemptive Story

The questions below are designed for children. Older groups may omit them.

LEADER   What do we celebrate during this season?

CHILDREN   Christ ascended to heaven and the Spirit came down to live in us.

LEADER   What happened when the Spirit came to earth?

CHILDREN   God created the church, a people who would be the presence of God on earth.

LEADER   Why has God created the church?

CHILDREN   To reconcile the world to God.

LEADER   We are a kingdom of priests. God designed us to reveal his character on earth.

If the questions are omitted, the liturgy continues here.

LEADER This season we celebrate Jesus' ascension and the coming of the Holy Spirit to God's people. Jesus had to leave that we might become the dwelling place of God through the presence of the Holy Spirit. Jesus told us that those who believe in him will do greater things than he did, because he returned to the Father.

Readings for the Season ✚

SUMMER HOME GATHERING—*THE CELEBRATION OF NEW LIFE*
See the liturgy for this home gathering on page 186.
Weekday liturgies for the week following Pentecost are found on page 155.

SECOND WEEK AFTER PENTECOST

Jesus came and said to the disciples: "All authority in heaven and on earth has been given to me. Go therefore and make disciples of all nations, baptizing them in the name of the Father and of the Son and of the Holy Spirit, teaching them to observe all that I have commanded you. And behold, I am with you always, to the end of the age." Matthew 28:18–20
Additional Reading: Matthew 28:16–20; Matthew 16:18–19
Weekday liturgies for this week are found on page 157.

THIRD WEEK AFTER PENTECOST[46]

The early church shared time, food, and resources: "They devoted themselves to the apostles' teaching and the fellowship, to the breaking of bread and the prayers. And awe came upon every soul, and many wonders and signs were being done through the apostles. And all who believed were together and had all things in common." Acts 2:42–44
Additional Reading: Acts 2:42–46
Weekday liturgies for this week are found on page 159.

FOURTH WEEK AFTER PENTECOST

The body of Christ is one body: "There is one body and one Spirit—just as you were called to the one hope that belongs to your call—one Lord, one faith, one baptism, one God and Father of all, who is over all and through all and in all." Ephesians 4:4–6
Additional Reading: Ephesians 4:1–6
Weekday liturgies for this week are found on page 161.

FIFTH WEEK AFTER PENTECOST

FIFTH WEEK AFTER PENTECOST

A promise was made thousands of years ago and when the Spirit came upon the church in Jerusalem, the promise was fulfilled. "You shall be my treasured possession among all peoples, for all the earth is mine; and you shall be to me a kingdom of priests and a holy nation." Exodus 19:5–6

Additional Reading: Exodus 19:1–6; Revelation 1:5–6
Weekday liturgies for this week are found on page 163.

SIXTH WEEK AFTER PENTECOST

Jesus is faithful to his bride: "I will betroth you to me in faithfulness. And you shall know the LORD. . . . And I will have mercy on No Mercy, and I will say to Not My People, 'You are my people'; and he shall say, 'You are my God.'" Hosea 2:20, 23

Additional Reading: Hosea 2:18–23
Weekday liturgies for this week are found on page 165.

SEVENTH WEEK AFTER PENTECOST

The last act witnesses a beautiful bride prepared for her husband: "I saw the holy city, new Jerusalem, coming down out of heaven from God, prepared as a bride adorned for her husband." Revelation 21:2

Additional Reading: Revelation 21:1–4
Weekday liturgies for this week are found on page 167.

ADDITIONAL Over dinner, older groups may want to engage in creative, explorative discussion of the Scriptures, in the ancient tradition of Midrash. See Appendix E.

Blessing the Cup

LEADER We praise you, God, King of the Universe, for you have given us the fruit of the vine. Father, because you have freed us by the blood of your Son, Jesus, you have made us a kingdom of priests.

The leader pours the wine or juice and passes the cup so everyone drinks.

Blessing the Bread and Oil

LEADER We praise you, God, King of the Universe, for you give us bread from the earth. Jesus, you are the bread of life. We have one bread and we are one body.

LEADER We also praise you, God, King of the Universe, for you give us this oil. Spirit, you came down from heaven to dwell in and among us. By your presence, you have made us the temple of God.

EVERYONE   We celebrate the birth, life, death, resurrection, ascension, and return of our King, Jesus Christ.

Everyone takes the bread, dips into the oil, and eats.

LEADER   During this season, we ask that you would bind us together as the body of Christ. May we express the love of Jesus Christ, our Savior, to each other and to all we encounter.

Song of Celebration ✚
Sing a song of your choice.

The Peace of Sabbath

LEADER   The peace of Christ be with you.

EVERYONE   And also with you.

All pass the peace of Christ.

THE CLOSING OF SABBATH FOR THE TIME OF THE CHURCH

The Greeting

LEADER   The Lord be with you.

EVERYONE   And also with you.

LEADER   When we are together, the Christ in me sees the Christ in you. Wherever we go, whatever we do, the ground we walk together is holy ground.

The Lighting of the Two Candles

The questions below are designed for children. Older groups may omit them.

LEADER   We part from the Sabbath ceremoniously, just as we welcomed it. This evening, we tell the conclusion of God's redemptive plan and celebrate our hope in its completion.

LEADER   What do the two candles symbolize?

CHILDREN   God has separated the holy from the common things.

LEADER   What has God set apart?

CHILDREN   God has set apart his people.

If the questions are omitted, the liturgy continues here.

LEADER Just as God has set apart the Sabbath in order to bless the working week, God has also set apart his people. He has called out his people, the church, to be a people of love. May the world know that we are followers of Jesus by the love we have for each other.

LEADER We praise you, God, King of the Universe, who created light. Ever-present Spirit, you remind us of Jesus' words and place in us hope and joy. Fill us with your love.

One of the participants lights the two candles.

Song for the Season ✠
Sing a song of your choice.

The Cup of Blessing
The leader lifts the cup for all to see.

LEADER We lift up the cup of salvation.

EVERYONE For salvation belongs to our God.

LEADER Father, your blessing be upon us now and forever.

The leader places the cup in a dish.

LEADER We praise you, God, King of the Universe, for you have given us the fruit of the vine and you generously pour out your blessing on us.

EVERYONE Fill our cups to overflowing.

LEADER May the blessing that you pour on us spill over into the lives of those around us.

A participant places the cup in a dish and fills the cup until it overflows, then pours the remaining wine or juice into a cup for each member.

Short Prayer for the Week

LEADER Though we know the truth of God's redemptive story, we often forget God. We become so accustomed to the world around us that we often blend in without thinking. These short prayers reconnect our spirits back to God's Spirit, asking him to tune our ears and refocus our attention to his work and our identity in Christ.

PENTECOST WEEKEND

Spirit of the risen Christ, enable us to explore the depths of your power.

SECOND WEEK AFTER PENTECOST

Holy Spirit, in the beginning, you hovered over creation. Renew our lives.

THIRD WEEK AFTER PENTECOST[47]

Holy Spirit, you led Christ into the desert; like him, assist us in proclaiming the kingdom.

FOURTH WEEK AFTER PENTECOST

Holy Spirit, you are always with us and in us. Breathe your life into us.

FIFTH WEEK AFTER PENTECOST

Jesus, grant your church unwavering commitment to the gospel in thought and life.

SIXTH WEEK AFTER PENTECOST

May your Holy Spirit provide us with reconciling words and healing hands.

SEVENTH WEEK AFTER PENTECOST

Holy Spirit, grant your people favor with those we encounter. Never let us be put to shame.

Conclusion of the Day of Rest

LEADER   We now depart from our day of rest. Tomorrow we return to work even as we anticipate God's overflowing blessing on our lives this week. In returning to our work, we also long for our next day of rest as we long for the final day of rest where we will enjoy a great banquet hosted by Jesus Christ our King.

MEMBER   God will prepare a feast with the best food and the greatest of aged wines.

LEADER   What do you think the great banquet will look like? What do you think we will eat? What will the music be like?

The participants imagine the great banquet.

A participant lights the incense and wafts it through the room.

LEADER   We praise you, God, King of the Universe, for you have given us our memories, our desires, and our senses. With great joy we remember the sweetness of this day of rest and anticipate the day of rest to come.

Blessing of the Week

LEADER   May the grace of Christ our Savior, the love of God our Father, and the fellowship of the Spirit be with us throughout this week and forevermore. *Amen.*

The Lighting of the Candle

LEADER Jesus said: "You are the light of the world."

A participant lights the candle for the season.[49]

MEMBER We praise you, God, King of the Universe, for you have given us Jesus Christ and his Holy Spirit, for our freedom, our salvation, and our participation in his divine life.

EVERYONE We praise you, God, Creator and Redeemer.

LEADER We praise you, God, King of the Universe, for you have given us this day of rest. May the light that we have lit remind us of the light of your presence, which illumines our lives. We come to you, Lord Christ, and find rest for our souls.

The Blessing

Families with children may want to insert a short prayer for each child here.

LEADER Father, we pray that you would protect and bless all who are in this home. Watch over us in the strength of your love. In this home, may we live in the peace of your kingdom and as your church may we bear witness to your glory wherever we go.

Song of Blessing ✠

The Lord bless you and keep you;
The Lord make his face shine upon you.
The Lord be gracious to you.
And give you his peace, forever.

Telling the Redemptive Story

The questions below are designed for children. Older groups may omit them.

LEADER What has Jesus told us to seek before we seek anything else?

CHILDREN The kingdom of God.

LEADER Is God's kingdom here on earth?

CHILDREN Yes, where God's people live in his love and peace.

LEADER Is God's kingdom complete here on earth?

CHILDREN No, the world is still fallen.

LEADER Will there be a time when God's kingdom is perfectly expressed here on earth?

CHILDREN Yes, when Jesus our King returns.

If the questions are omitted, the liturgy continues here.

LEADER   This season we celebrate the kingdom of God. Though we only experience tastes of his kingdom here on earth, with hope we choose to seek God's kingdom first above all else. We look forward to the day when our King returns to establish his peaceable kingdom forever.

Readings for the Season ✠

FIRST WEEK OF THE TIME OF THE KINGDOM[50]

Jesus taught us, saying: "Seek first the kingdom of God and his righteousness, and all these things will be added to you." Matthew 6:33

> *Additional Reading: Matthew 6:33–34*
> *Weekday liturgies for this week are found on page 169.*

SECOND WEEK OF THE TIME OF THE KINGDOM

The people wanted a king other than God himself. They told Samuel: "'Give us a king to judge us.' . . . And the LORD said to Samuel, 'Obey the voice of the people . . . for they have not rejected you, but they have rejected me from being king over them.'" I Samuel 8:6–7

> *Additional Reading: 1 Samuel 8:1–9*
> *Weekday liturgies for this week are found on page 171.*

THIRD WEEK OF THE TIME OF THE KINGDOM

A promise was given to David: "I will set up one of your descendants after you, who will be of your sons; and I will establish his kingdom. I will be his father and he shall be my son. . . . I will settle him in my house and in my kingdom forever, and his throne shall be established forever." I Chronicles 17:11, 13–14 (NASB)

> *Additional Reading: 1 Chronicles 17:3–15*
> *Weekday liturgies for this week are found on page 173.*

FOURTH WEEK OF THE TIME OF THE KINGDOM

Daniel saw a vision of a man presented to God, the Ancient of Days: "And to him was given dominion and glory and a kingdom, that all peoples, nations, and languages might serve him; his dominion is an everlasting dominion, which shall not pass away, and his kingdom is one which will not be destroyed." Daniel 7:14

> *Additional Reading: Daniel 7:13–14*
> *Weekday liturgies for this week are found on page 174.*

FIFTH WEEK OF THE TIME OF THE KINGDOM

Jesus talked about the kingdom in parables: "The kingdom of heaven is like a grain of mustard seed that a man took and sowed in his field. It is the smallest of all seeds, but when it has grown it is larger than all the garden plants and becomes a tree, so that the birds of the air come and make nests in its branches." Matthew 13:31–32

Additional Reading: Matthew 13:31–35
Weekday liturgies for this week are found on page 176.

SIXTH WEEK OF THE TIME OF THE KINGDOM

Jesus said: "The kingdom of God is as if a man should scatter seed on the ground. He sleeps and rises night and day, and the seed sprouts and grows; he knows not how." Mark 4:26–27

Additional Reading: Mark 4:26–29
Weekday liturgies for this week are found on page 178.

SEVENTH WEEK OF THE TIME OF THE KINGDOM

Jesus told us: "The kingdom of heaven is like treasure hidden in a field. When a man found it, he hid it again, and then in his joy went and sold all he had and bought that field." Matthew 13:44 (NIV)

Additional Reading: Matthew 13:24–46
Weekday liturgies for this week are found on page 180.

EIGHTH WEEK OF THE TIME OF THE KINGDOM

The apostle Peter wrote: "You are a chosen race, a royal priesthood, a holy nation, a people for his own possession, that you may proclaim the excellencies of him who called you out of darkness into his marvelous light." 1 Peter 2:9

Additional Reading: 1 Peter 2:4–12
Weekday liturgies for this week are found on page 182.

NINTH WEEK OF THE TIME OF THE KINGDOM[51]

The Pharisees asked Jesus when the kingdom of God would come. He answered them: "The kingdom of God is not coming with signs to be observed, nor will they say, 'Look, here it is!' or 'There!' for behold, the kingdom of God is in the midst of you." Luke 17:20–21

Additional Reading: Luke 17:20–33
Weekday liturgies for this week are found on page 184.

Blessing the Cup

LEADER   We praise you, God, King of the Universe, for you have given us the fruit of the vine. Father, because you have freed us by the blood of your Son, Jesus, you have made us a kingdom of priests.

The leader pours the wine or juice and passes the cup so everyone drinks.

152

Blessing the Bread and Oil

LEADER We praise you, God, King of the Universe, for you give us bread from the earth. Jesus, we remember your words that your banquet table welcomes the poor. "Blessed is everyone who eats bread in the kingdom of God."

LEADER We also praise you, God, King of the Universe, for you give us this oil. Spirit, you have entrusted the mystery of the kingdom of God to us. Teach us to welcome the kingdom, as trusting children.

EVERYONE We celebrate the birth, life, death, resurrection, ascension, and return of our King, Jesus Christ.

Everyone takes the bread, dips into the oil, and eats.

LEADER During this season, we pray God's kingdom come and his will be done on earth as it is in heaven. May the kingdom of God penetrate the deepest recesses of our hearts and spread to the farthest parts of the earth.

Song of Celebration ✠

Sing a song of your choice.

The Peace of Sabbath

LEADER The peace of Christ be with you.

EVERYONE And also with you.

All pass the peace of Christ.

THE CLOSING OF SABBATH FOR THE TIME OF THE KINGDOM

The Greeting

LEADER The Lord be with you.

EVERYONE And also with you.

LEADER When we are together, the Christ in me sees the Christ in you. Wherever we go, whatever we do, the ground we walk together is holy ground.

The Lighting of the Two Candles

The questions below are designed for children. Older groups may omit them.

LEADER We part from the Sabbath ceremoniously, just as we welcomed it. This evening, we tell the conclusion of God's redemptive plan and celebrate our hope in its completion.

LEADER	What do the two candles symbolize?
CHILDREN	The kingdom of God and the kingdom of Man.
LEADER	How does the kingdom of God relate to the kingdom of man?
CHILDREN	Through his people, God establishes his kingdom that we might redeem the kingdom of man with humility, love, and peace.

If the questions are omitted, the liturgy continues here.

LEADER	God has sent his Spirit that his people might live the kingdom of God here on earth. Though we do not express his kingdom perfectly, we look forward to a day when God's kingdom of peace will be established forever.
LEADER	We praise you, God, King of the Universe, who created light. May the light of your kingdom illumine our lives, both now and forever. *Amen.* *One of the participants lights the two candles.*

Song for the Season ✠

Sing a song of your choice.

The Cup of Blessing

The leader lifts the cup for all to see.

LEADER	We lift up the cup of salvation.
EVERYONE	For salvation belongs to our God.
LEADER	Father, your blessing be upon us now and forever.
	The leader places the cup in a dish.
LEADER	We praise you, God, King of the Universe, for you have given us the fruit of the vine and you generously pour out your blessing on us.
EVERYONE	Fill our cups to overflowing.
LEADER	May the blessing that you pour on us spill over into the lives of those around us.
	A participant places the cup in a dish and fills the cup until it overflows, then pours the remaining wine or juice into a cup for each member.

Short Prayer for the Week

LEADER	Though we know the truth of God's redemptive story, we often forget God. We become so accustomed to the world around us that we often blend in without thinking. These short prayers reconnect our spirits back to God's Spirit, asking him to tune our ears and refocus our attention on the reality of his kingdom.

FIRST WEEK OF THE TIME OF THE KINGDOM[52]
Make us one, God, as you, Father, Son, and Spirit are one.

SECOND WEEK OF THE TIME OF THE KINGDOM
Lord Christ, take our weaknesses and make them your strengths.

THIRD WEEK OF THE TIME OF THE KINGDOM
Your presence within us offers unconditional forgiveness and trust.

FOURTH WEEK OF THE TIME OF THE KINGDOM
Grant your church an unwavering commitment to the gospel in thought and life.

FIFTH WEEK OF THE TIME OF THE KINGDOM
Spirit, teach us to receive the kingdom of God as a child.

SIXTH WEEK OF THE TIME OF THE KINGDOM
Christ Jesus, encourage your people to enjoy the beauty of redemption.

SEVENTH WEEK OF THE TIME OF THE KINGDOM
Jesus, rid us of our worries and replace them with the peace of childlike trust.

EIGHTH WEEK OF THE TIME OF THE KINGDOM
Christ Jesus, you always come to us wherever we may be.

NINTH WEEK OF THE TIME OF THE KINGDOM[53]
Spirit of life, lead me and teach me to trust you—even when I am in darkness.

Conclusion of the Day of Rest

LEADER   We now depart from our day of rest. Tomorrow we must return to work. May the blessings of God flow in our lives and may the kingdom of God invade all that we do, as we look forward to the day when his kingdom is established forever. *Amen.*

MEMBER   God will prepare a feast with the best food and the greatest of aged wines, and his kingdom will have no end.

LEADER   What do you think the great banquet will look like? What do you think we will eat? What will the music be like?
The participants imagine the great banquet.
A participant lights the incense and wafts it through the room.

LEADER   We praise you, God, King of the Universe, for you have given us our memories, our desires, and our senses. With great joy we remember the sweetness of this day of rest and anticipate the day of rest to come.

Blessing of the Week

LEADER   May the kingdom of God reign in our homes, in our hearts, and in our lives. *Amen.*

The Lighting of the Candle

The leader prays as a participant lights the candle.

LEADER Let us pray. Holy Spirit, light of all who believe, enlighten us and renew our home and community in the fire of your love.

Meditation or Silence[54] ✚

After a moment of silence or a physical expression of prayer, the leader continues.

LEADER Spirit, your presence is with us wherever we go.

Psalm

MONDAY • Psalm 113 and 114   **TUESDAY** • Psalm 115   **WEDNESDAY** • Psalm 116
THURSDAY • Psalm 117   **FRIDAY** • Psalm 118

Song for the Season ✚

Sing a song of your choice.

Short Verse

READER The apostle Paul wrote: "If the Spirit of him who raised Jesus from the dead dwells in you, he who raised Christ Jesus from the dead will also give life to your mortal bodies through his Spirit who dwells in you." Romans 8:11

Short Prayer

READER Spirit of the risen Christ, enable us to explore the depths of your power.

Scripture Reading

EVERYONE Father, open our eyes that we might see the wonders of your truth.

MONDAY

Moses told God: "If your presence will not go with me, do not bring us up from here." Exodus 33:15

Additional Reading: Exodus 33:12–23

TUESDAY

The risen Christ said to the disciples: "Peace be with you. As the Father sent me, so am I sending you." Then he breathed on them and said, "Receive the Holy Spirit." John 20:21–22

Additional Reading: John 20:19–23
WEDNESDAY

The apostle Paul wrote: "We all, with unveiled face, beholding the glory of the Lord, are being transformed into the same image from one degree of glory to another. For this comes from the Lord who is the Spirit." 2 Corinthians 3:18

Additional Reading: 2 Corinthians 3:12–18

THURSDAY

Paul wrote: "But when the goodness and loving kindness of God our Savior appeared, he saved us, not because of works done by us in righteousness, but according to his own mercy, by the washing of regeneration and renewal of the Holy Spirit, whom he poured out on us richly through Jesus Christ our Savior, so that being justified by his grace we might become heirs according to the hope of eternal life." Titus 3:4–7

Additional Reading: Titus 3:4–11

FRIDAY

Though they came from all over the world, when the Spirit descended the people became one: "And it shall come to pass that everyone who calls upon the name of the Lord shall be saved." Acts 2:21

Additional Reading: Acts 2:1–6, 14–17, 21

Open Intercession or Daily Intercession
For daily intercessions see Appendix F.

Prayer for the Week

Let us pray that the flame of the Spirit will descend upon us. Father in heaven, these fifty days we have celebrated the mystery of your revealed love. Here we are, your people gathered in prayer, open to receive the Spirit's flame. May it come to rest in our hearts and homes and disperse any divisions of word and deed. With one voice and one song may we praise your name in joy and thanksgiving. Grant this through Christ our Lord. Amen. —*Based on a prayer from the New Saint Joseph Missal*

Song for the Season
Sing a song of your choice.

The Lighting of the Candle

The leader prays as a participant lights the candle.

LEADER   Let us pray. Holy Spirit, light of all who believe, enlighten us and renew our home and community in the fire of your love.

Meditation or Silence ✚

After a moment of silence or a physical expression of prayer, the leader continues.

LEADER   Spirit, you have made us for freedom.

Psalm

MONDAY • Psalm 145:1–9   TUESDAY • Psalm 146   WEDNESDAY • Psalm 147

THURSDAY • Psalm 148   FRIDAY • Psalm 149 and 150

Song for the Season ✚

Sing a song of your choice.

Short Verse

READER   Jesus' great commission is this: "Go therefore and make disciples of all nations, baptizing them in the name of the Father and of the Son and of the Holy Spirit, teaching them to observe all that I have commanded you. And behold, I am with you always, to the end of the age." Matthew 28:19–20

Short Prayer

READER   Holy Spirit, in the beginning, you hovered over creation. Renew our lives.

Scripture Reading

EVERYONE   Father, open our eyes that we might see the wonders of your truth.

MONDAY

From the relationship of the man and the woman, God would tell the entire story of redemption—he the groom and his people the bride: "God created man in his own image, in the image of God he created him; male and female he created them." Genesis 1:27

Additional Reading: Genesis 2:18–25

158

TUESDAY

God said: "I will take you to be my people, and I will be your God." From the beginning God has desired to dwell with his people. Exodus 6:7

Additional Reading: Exodus 6:7–8

WEDNESDAY

God's story is one of love. The Father sent his Son to pursue a bride. With a costly gift he has pledged his undying love for her. The bridegroom goes to prepare a home and he will return for his bride. Jesus said: "I am going [to my Father's house] to prepare a place for you. And if I go and prepare a place for you, I will come back and take you to be with me that you also may be where I am." John 14:2b–3 (NIV)

Additional Reading: Song of Solomon 4:9–16

THURSDAY

Even though his beloved was unfaithful, God remained true. To his people he said: "I will betroth you to me in faithfulness. And you shall know the Lord." Hosea 2:20

Additional Reading: Hosea 2:14–23

FRIDAY

The end of the story sees the City of God descending to earth: "I saw the holy city, new Jerusalem, coming down out of heaven from God, prepared as a bride adorned for her husband." Revelation 21:2

Additional Reading: Revelation 21:1–2

Open Intercession or Daily Intercession
For daily intercessions see Appendix F.

Prayer for the Week

God of delight, Wisdom sings your Word at the crossroads where humanity and divinity meet. Invite us into your joyful being where you know and are known in each beginning, in all sustenance, in every redemption, that we may manifest your unity in the diverse ministries you entrust to us, truly reflecting your triune majesty in the faith that acts, in the hope that does not disappoint, and in the love that endures. *Amen. —Based on a prayer from the* Revised Common Lectionary

Song for the Season ✚
Sing a song of your choice.

The Lighting of the Candle

The leader prays as a participant lights the candle.

LEADER   Let us pray. Holy Spirit, light of all who believe, enlighten us and renew our home and community in the fire of your love.

Meditation or Silence ✛

After a moment of silence or a physical expression of prayer, the leader continues.

LEADER   Spirit, you bring us together in your love.

Psalm

MONDAY • Psalm 104:30–34 TUESDAY • Psalm 33:1–7
WEDNESDAY • Psalm 20:6–9
THURSDAY • Psalm 9:7–10 FRIDAY • Psalm 62:5–8

Song for the Season ✛

Sing a song of your choice.

Short Verse

READER   The early church lived in the unity of the Spirit: "They devoted themselves to the apostles' teaching and the fellowship, to the breaking of bread and the prayers." Acts 2:42

Short Prayer

READER   Holy Spirit, you led Christ into the desert; like him, assist us in proclaiming the kingdom.

Scripture Reading

EVERYONE   Father, open our eyes that we might see the wonders of your truth.

MONDAY

Jesus told Thomas: "Have you believed because you have seen me? Blessed are those who have not seen and yet have believed." John 20:29

Additional Reading: John 20:24–29

TUESDAY

The apostle John wrote: "No one has ever seen God; if we love one another, God abides in us and his love is perfected in us." 1 John 4:12

Additional Reading: 1 John 4:12–21

WEDNESDAY

Jesus said: "When the Spirit of truth comes, he will guide you into all the truth, for he will not speak on his own authority, but whatever he hears he will speak." John 16:13

Additional Reading: John 16:12–15

THURSDAY

Peter wrote: "Though you have not seen him, you love him. Though you do not now see him, you believe in him and rejoice with joy that is inexpressible and filled with glory." 1 Peter 1:8

Additional Reading: 1 Peter 1:3–9

FRIDAY

Jesus said: "Peace I leave with you; my peace I give you. I do not give to you as the world gives. Do not let your hearts be troubled and do not be afraid." John 14:27 (NIV)

Additional Reading: John 14:22–26

Open Intercession or Daily Intercession
For daily intercessions see Appendix F.

Prayer for the Week

As I rise I thank you, O Holy Trinity, for your great goodness and patience. Enlighten my mind and open my mouth that I may meditate on your words, and understand your commandments, and do your will, and sing to you in heartfelt confession, and sing praises to your all-holy name: of the Father, and of the Son, and of the Holy Spirit, now and ever, and unto the ages of ages.

O come, let us worship God, our King.

O come, let us worship and fall down before Christ himself, our King and God. Amen. —*Based on a prayer of St. Basil the Great*

Song for the Season ✠
Sing a song of your choice.

Note: If the preceding Sabbath was celebrated on the first weekend of July, move to the weekly liturgies for the Time of the Kingdom, located on page 169.

The Lighting of the Candle

The leader prays as a participant lights the candle.

LEADER   Let us pray. Holy Spirit, light of all who believe, enlighten us and renew our home and community in the fire of your love.

Meditation or Silence ✦

After a moment of silence or a physical expression of prayer, the leader continues.

LEADER   Holy Spirit, you bring us your help and your comfort.

Psalm

MONDAY • Psalm 139:1–12 TUESDAY • Psalm 48:1–8 WEDNESDAY • Psalm 131:1–3
THURSDAY • Psalm 45:10–15 FRIDAY • Psalm 90:1–6

Song for the Season ✦

Sing a song of your choice.

Short Verse

READER   The psalmist wrote: "For God is the King of all the earth; sing praises with a psalm!" Psalm 47:7

Short Prayer

READER   Holy Spirit, you are always with us and in us. Breathe your life into us.

Scripture Reading

EVERYONE   Father, open our eyes that we might see the wonders of your truth.

MONDAY

The Holy Spirit is our helper: "The Spirit helps us in our weakness. We do not know what we ought to pray for, but the Spirit himself intercedes for us with groans that words cannot express." Romans 8:26 (NIV)

Additional Reading: Romans 8:26–27

TUESDAY

Isaiah told of God's relationship to his people: "For your Maker is your husband, the Lord of hosts is his name; and the Holy One of Israel is your Redeemer, the God of the whole earth he is called." Isaiah 54:5

Additional Reading: Isaiah 54:5–10

WEDNESDAY

Peter told the religious leaders: "The God of our fathers raised Jesus, whom you killed by hanging him on a tree. . . . And we are witnesses to these things, and so is the Holy Spirit, whom God has given to those who obey him." Acts 5:30, 32

Additional Reading: Acts 5:17–33

THURSDAY

Paul told the believers to endure in the Spirit: "The one who sows to the Spirit will from the Spirit reap eternal life. And let us not grow weary of doing good, for in due season we will reap, if we do not give up." Galatians 6:8–9

Additional Reading: Galatians 6:7–10

FRIDAY

God promised to set the captives free: "And I will make all my mountains a road, and my highways shall be raised up." Isaiah 49:11

Additional Reading: Isaiah 49:8–13

Open Intercession or Daily Intercession

For daily intercessions see Appendix F.

Prayer for the Week

Holy Spirit, in every situation we would like to welcome you with great simplicity. And it is above all by the intelligence of the heart that you enable us to penetrate the mystery of your life within us. *Amen. —Based on a prayer from the Taizé Community*

Song for the Season ✠

Sing a song of your choice.

Note: If the preceding Sabbath was celebrated on the first weekend of July, move to the weekly liturgies for the Time of the Kingdom on page 169.[55]

The Lighting of the Candle

The leader prays as a participant lights the candle.

LEADER   Let us pray. Holy Spirit, light of all who believe, enlighten us and renew our home and community in the fire of your love.

Meditation or Silence ✠

After a moment of silence or a physical expression of prayer, the leader continues.

LEADER   Spirit, you cover us in your presence.

Psalm

MONDAY • Psalm 17:1–7   TUESDAY • Psalm 33:1–9   WEDNESDAY • Psalm 123:1–2
THURSDAY • Psalm 105:1–6   FRIDAY • Psalm 104:16–24

Song for the Season ✠

Sing a song of your choice.

Short Verse

READER   "Great salvation he brings to his king, and shows steadfast love to his anointed, to David and his offspring forever." Psalm 18:50

Short Prayer

READER   Grant your church an unwavering commitment to the gospel in thought and life.

Scripture Reading

EVERYONE   Father, open our eyes that we might see the wonders of your truth.

MONDAY

Joel instructed the people: "Rend your heart and not your garments. Return to the LORD your God, for he is gracious and merciful, slow to anger and abounding in steadfast love." Joel 2:13

Additional Reading: Joel 2:12–13

TUESDAY

God said: "I have put my words in your mouth and covered you in the shadow of my hand, establishing the heavens and laying the foundations of the earth, and saying to Zion, 'You are my people.'" Isaiah 51:16

Additional Reading: Isaiah 51:11–16

WEDNESDAY

God said: "I have blotted out your transgressions like a cloud and your sins like mist; return to me, for I have redeemed you." Isaiah 44:22

Additional Reading: Isaiah 44:21–28

THURSDAY

Jesus said: "Heaven and earth will pass away, but my words will not pass away." Matthew 24:35

Additional Reading: Matthew 24:32–35

FRIDAY

Paul encouraged the believers in Rome: "And hope does not put us to shame, because God's love has been poured into our hearts through the Holy Spirit who has been given to us." Romans 5:5

Additional Reading: Romans 5:1–11

Open Intercession or Daily Intercession
For daily intercessions see Appendix F.

Prayer for the Week

Almighty God, who on the day of Pentecost opened the way of the divine life to every nation by the promised gift of your Holy Spirit, spread throughout the world the good news of redemption and restoration that it may reach to the ends of the earth; through Jesus Christ our Lord, who lives and reigns with you, in the unity of the Holy Spirit, one God, now and forevermore. Amen. *—Based on a prayer from the Book of Common Prayer, 1979*

Song for the Season
Sing a song of your choice.

Note: If the preceding Sabbath was celebrated on the first weekend of July, move to the weekly liturgies for the Time of the Kingdom on page 169.[56]

The Lighting of the Candle

The leader prays as a participant lights the candle.

LEADER   Let us pray. Holy Spirit, light of all who believe, enlighten us and renew our home and community in the fire of your love.

Meditation or Silence ✥

After a moment of silence or a physical expression of prayer, the leader continues.

LEADER   Spirit, you generously welcome us in your presence.

Psalm

MONDAY • Psalm 146:1–7   **TUESDAY** • Psalm 8:1–9   **WEDNESDAY** • Psalm 42:1–5
THURSDAY • Psalm 52:6–9   **FRIDAY** • Psalm 85:8–13

Song for the Season ✥

Sing a song of your choice.

Short Verse

READER   Of Jesus it is written: "On his robe and on his thigh he has a name written, King of kings and Lord of lords." Revelation 19:16

Short Prayer

READER   May your Holy Spirit provide us with reconciling words and healing hands.

Scripture Reading

EVERYONE   Father, open our eyes that we might see the wonders of your truth.

MONDAY

Paul reminded us: "God was reconciling the world to himself, not counting their trespasses against them, and entrusting to us the message of reconciliation." 2 Corinthians 5:19

Additional Reading: 2 Corinthians 5:18–21

TUESDAY

Zechariah prophesied: "On that day there shall be a fountain opened for the house of David and the inhabitants of Jerusalem, to cleanse them from sin and uncleanness." Zechariah 13:1

Additional Reading: Zechariah 13:1–2

WEDNESDAY

This is how you can recognize the Spirit of God: "Every spirit that confesses that Jesus Christ has come in the flesh is from God." 1 John 4:2

Additional Reading: 1 John 4:1–4

THURSDAY

The apostle Paul made this resolution: "For I decided to know nothing among you except Jesus Christ and him crucified." 1 Corinthians 2:2

Additional Reading: 1 Corinthians 2:1–3

FRIDAY

The Scriptures tell us: "If any of you lacks wisdom, let him ask God, who gives generously to all without reproach, and it will be given him." James 1:5

Additional Reading: James 1:2–18

Open Intercession or Daily Intercession

For daily intercessions see Appendix F.

Prayer for the Week

Come Holy Spirit, fill the hearts of your faithful and kindle in them the fire of your love. Send forth your Spirit and all shall be created and you shall renew the face of the earth.

O God, who by the light of the Holy Spirit, did instruct the hearts of the faithful, grant that by the same Holy Spirit we may be truly wise and ever rejoice in his consolations, through Christ our Lord. *Amen. —Based on a traditional Catholic novena to the Holy Spirit*

Song for the Season ✠

Sing a song of your choice.

Note: If the preceding Sabbath was celebrated on the first weekend of July, move to the weekly liturgies for the Time of the Kingdom on page 169.[57]

The Lighting of the Candle

The leader prays as a participant lights the candle.

LEADER   Let us pray. Holy Spirit, light of all who believe, enlighten us and renew our home and community in the fire of your love.

Meditation or Silence ✛

After a moment of silence or a physical expression of prayer, the leader continues.

LEADER   Spirit, you produce in us what we cannot produce in ourselves.

Psalm

MONDAY • Psalm 50:1–6   **TUESDAY** • Psalm 80:1–3   **WEDNESDAY** • Psalm 71:12–16   **THURSDAY** • Psalm 81:1–10   **FRIDAY** • Psalm 139:13–18

Song for the Season ✛

Sing a song of your choice.

Short Verse

READER   Paul writes: "The fruit of the Spirit is love, joy, peace, patience, kindness, goodness, faithfulness, gentleness, self-control; against such things there is no law." Galatians 5:22–23

Short Prayer

READER   Holy Spirit, grant your people favor with those we encounter. Never let us be put to shame.

Scripture Reading

EVERYONE   Father, open our eyes that we might see the wonders of your truth.

MONDAY

Isaiah saw God in his holiness and instantly understood his own sinfulness. Yet, the exalted God reached down to him and restored him: "Behold, this has touched your lips; your guilt is taken away, and your sin atoned for." Isaiah 6:7

Additional Reading: Isaiah 6:1–8

TUESDAY

The gospel is powerful, revealing God's righteousness. Graciously, God welcomes us to live in his righteousness through faith: "The righteous shall live by faith." Romans 1:17

Additional Reading: Romans 1:8–17

WEDNESDAY

Isaiah longed for God: "My soul yearns for you in the night; my spirit within me earnestly seeks you." Isaiah 26:9

Additional Reading: Isaiah 26:7–9

THURSDAY

Our confidence in the faith and our endurance will be richly rewarded, for the just will live by faith: "My righteous one shall live by faith." Hebrews 10:38

Additional Reading: Hebrews 10:32–39

FRIDAY

Through Jesus' death we have new life: "For the death he died he died to sin, once for all, but the life he lives he lives to God. So you also must consider yourselves dead to sin and alive to God in Christ Jesus." Romans 6:10–11

Additional Reading: Romans 6:3–11

Open Intercession or Daily Intercession
For daily intercessions see Appendix F.

Prayer for the Week
Breathe into me, Holy Spirit, that my thoughts may all be holy. Move in me, Holy Spirit, that my work, too, may be holy. Attract my heart, Holy Spirit, that I may love only what is holy. Strengthen me, Holy Spirit, that I may defend all that is holy. Protect me, Holy Spirit, that I may always be holy. Amen. —*Based on a prayer of St. Augustine*

Song for the Season ✠
Sing a song of your choice.

The Lighting of the Candle

The leader prays as a participant lights the candle.[59]

LEADER Let us pray. Spirit of God, come and empower your church. May we be a shining light, a city on a hill, dispelling darkness wherever we go.

Meditation or Silence ✚

After a moment of silence or a physical expression of prayer, the leader continues.

LEADER Spirit, you bring unity from our diversity.

Psalm

MONDAY • Psalm 87 **TUESDAY** • Psalm 133:1–3 **WEDNESDAY** • Psalm 68:24–35
THURSDAY • Psalm 3:3–4, 7–8 **FRIDAY** • Psalm 47:1–9

Song for the Season ✚

Sing a song of your choice.

Short Verse

READER Of the church it is said: "There is one body and one Spirit—just as you were called to the one hope that belongs to your call—one Lord, one faith, one baptism." Ephesians 4:4–5

Short Prayer

READER Make us one, God, as you—Father, Son, and Spirit—are one.

Scripture Reading

EVERYONE Father, open our eyes that we might see the wonders of your truth.

MONDAY

The early church was committed to the gospel and to each other: "They devoted themselves to the apostles' teaching and the fellowship, to the breaking of bread and the prayers." Acts 2:42

Additional Reading: Acts 2:42–46

TUESDAY

Though different in role and capabilities, the members of the body function as one: "The body is a unit, though it is made up of many parts; and though all its parts are many, they form one body. So it is with Christ. For we were all baptized by one

Spirit into one body." I Corinthians 12:12–13 (NIV)

Additional Reading: 1 Corinthians 12:4–7, 12–13

WEDNESDAY

We need each other for a whole and fruitful life: "In Christ we who are many form one body, and each member belongs to all the others." Romans 12:5 (NIV)

Additional Reading: Romans 12:1–21

THURSDAY

The kingdom of God is expressed when the body lives as one: "There is one body and one Spirit—just as you were called to one hope when you were called—one Lord, one faith, one baptism; one God and Father of all, who is over all and through all and in all." Ephesians 4:4–6 (NIV)

Additional Reading: Ephesians 4:1–16

FRIDAY

Jesus prayed for us: "May they be brought to complete unity to let the world know that you sent me and have loved them even as you have loved me." John 17:23 (NIV)

Additional Reading: John 17:6–24

Open Intercession or Daily Intercession
For daily intercessions see Appendix F.

Prayer for the Week

O Holy Spirit, my God, I adore you, and acknowledge, here in your divine presence, that I am nothing and can do nothing without you. Come, great helper, father of the poor, comforter, fulfill the promise of our Savior, who did not leave us orphans, and grant that I may participate in those gifts that you give so freely, and with so much mercy and generosity.

Take from my heart whatever is not pleasing to you, and make of it a worthy dwelling place for you. Illumine my mind, that I may see and understand the things that are for my eternal good.

Inflame my heart with pure love for you, that I may be cleansed from the distractions of the world, and that my whole life may be hidden with Jesus in God. Strengthen my will, that I may be made conformable to your divine will, and be guided by your leadership. *Amen. —Based on a novena to the Holy Spirit*

Song for the Season ✠
Sing a song of your choice.

The Lighting of the Candle

The leader prays as a participant lights the candle.

LEADER   Let us pray. Spirit of God, come and empower your church. May we be a shining light, a city on a hill, dispelling darkness wherever we go.

Meditation or Silence

After a moment of silence or a physical expression of prayer, the leader continues.

LEADER   Holy Spirit, in you we find our consolation.

Psalm

MONDAY • Psalm 27:1–8 TUESDAY • Psalm 63:1–8 WEDNESDAY • Psalm 34:1–3
THURSDAY • Psalm 71:1–3 FRIDAY • Psalm 96:1–6

Song for the Season

Sing a song of your choice.

Short Verse

READER   Jesus prayed: "I do not ask for these only, but also for those who will believe in me through their word, that they may all be one, just as you, Father, are in me, and I in you, that they also may be in us, so that the world may believe that you have sent me." John 17:20–21

Short Prayer

READER   Lord Christ, take our weaknesses and make them your strengths.

Scripture Reading

EVERYONE   Father, open our eyes that we might see the wonders of your truth.

MONDAY

Jesus said: "Truly, I say to you, there is no one who has left house or brothers or sisters or mother or father or children or lands, for my sake and for the gospel, who will not receive a hundredfold now in this time, houses and brothers and sisters and mothers and children and lands, with persecutions, and in the age to come eternal life." Mark 10:29–30

Additional Reading: Mark 10:23–31

172

TUESDAY

Jesus told us of worshipers the Father desires: "True worshipers will worship the Father in spirit and truth, for the Father is seeking such people to worship him." John 4:23

Additional Reading: John 4:23–26

WEDNESDAY

The prophet reminded us that God is holy and is to be revered: "But the Lord is in his holy temple; let all the earth keep silence before him." Habakkuk 2:20

Additional Reading: Habakkuk 2:2–4, 20

THURSDAY

He is our God and we are his people: "Oh come, let us worship and bow down; let us kneel before the Lord, our Maker! For he is our God, and we are the people of his pasture." Psalm 95:6–7

Additional Reading: Psalm 95:1–7

FRIDAY

Paul was unwaveringly committed to following Jesus: "I count everything as loss because of the surpassing worth of knowing Christ Jesus my Lord. For his sake I have suffered the loss of all things." Philippians 3:8

Additional Reading: Philippians 3:7–11

Open Intercession or Daily Intercession

For daily intercessions see Appendix F.

Prayer for the Week

Jesus, our peace, if our lips keep silence, our heart listens to you and also speaks to you. And you say to each one of us: surrender yourself in all simplicity to the life of the Holy Spirit; for this, the little bit of faith you have is enough. *Amen. —Based on a prayer of the Taizé Community*

Song for the Season 🕂

Sing a song of your choice.

The Lighting of the Candle
The leader prays as a participant lights the candle.

LEADER   Let us pray. Spirit of God, come and empower your church. May we be a shining light, a city on a hill, dispelling darkness wherever we go.

Meditation or Silence ✚
After a moment of silence or a physical expression of prayer, the leader continues.

LEADER   Spirit, you make our lives a living expression of Christ.

Psalm

MONDAY • Psalm 103:1–5   TUESDAY • Psalm 103:6–14

WEDNESDAY • Psalm 103:15–22   THURSDAY • Psalm 126:1–6   FRIDAY • Psalm 46:1–11

Song for the Season ✚
Sing a song of your choice.

Short Verse

READER   God promised: "You shall be to me a kingdom of priests and a holy nation. These are the words that you shall speak to the people of Israel." Exodus 19:6

Short Prayer

READER   Your presence within us offers unconditional forgiveness and trust.

Scripture Reading

EVERYONE   Father, open our eyes that we might see the wonders of your truth.

MONDAY

Jesus said: "Let him who is without sin among you be the first to throw a stone." John 8:7

Additional Reading: John 8:1–11

TUESDAY

Jesus said: "'I tell you, her sins, which are many, are forgiven—for she loved much. But he who is forgiven little, loves little.' And he said to her, 'Your sins are forgiven.'" Luke 7:47–48

Additional Reading: Luke 7:36–50

WEDNESDAY

When Jesus saw the faith of his friends, he healed the paralytic and said: "Take heart, my son; your sins are forgiven." Matthew 9:2

Additional Reading: Matthew 9:1–8

THURSDAY

Paul wrote: "We are therefore Christ's ambassadors, as though God were making his appeal through us. We implore you on Christ's behalf: Be reconciled to God." 2 Corinthians 5:20 (NIV)

Additional Reading: 2 Corinthians 5:16–21

FRIDAY

God's people are a people of peace: "Put on then, as God's chosen ones, holy and beloved, compassionate hearts, kindness, humility, meekness, and patience." Colossians 3:12

Additional Reading: Colossians 3:12–17

Open Intercession or Daily Intercession
For daily intercessions see Appendix F.

Prayer for the Week

We praise you, O almighty and eternal God, for through Jesus Christ you have revealed your glory to all nations, to preserve the works of your mercy, that your church, being spread through the whole world, may continue with unchanging faith in the confession of your name. *Amen.* —*Based on a prayer of Archbishop John Carroll, 1791*

Song for the Season
Sing a song of your choice.

FOURTH WEEK OF THE TIME OF THE KINGDOM

The Lighting of the Candle
The leader prays as a participant lights the candle.

LEADER Let us pray. Spirit of God, come and empower your church. May we be a shining light, a city on a hill, dispelling darkness wherever we go.

Meditation or Silence ✠

After a moment of silence or a physical expression of prayer, the leader continues.

LEADER   Holy Spirit, we find peace knowing that you pray within us.

Psalm

MONDAY • Psalm 86:1–13   TUESDAY • Psalm 45:1–7   WEDNESDAY • Psalm 48:9–14
THURSDAY • Psalm 1:1–6   FRIDAY • Psalm 4:6–8

Song for the Season ✠

Sing a song of your choice.

Short Verse

READER   Jesus looked at people and said: "With man it is impossible, but not with God. For all things are possible with God." Mark 10:27

Short Prayer

READER   Grant your church an unwavering commitment to the gospel in thought and life.

Scripture Reading

EVERYONE   Father, open our eyes that we might see the wonders of your truth.

MONDAY

God is our light: "The LORD will be your everlasting light, and your God will be your glory." Isaiah 60:19
Additional Reading: Isaiah 60:19–22

TUESDAY

The author of Hebrews encouraged us: "Jesus Christ is the same yesterday and today and forever." Hebrews 13:8
Additional Reading: Hebrews 13:1–8

WEDNESDAY

We have one bread and we are one body: "The bread that we break, is it not a participation in the body of Christ? Because there is one bread, we who are many are one body." 1 Corinthians 10:16–17
Additional Reading: 1 Corinthians 10:14–17

THURSDAY

The Scriptures are the standard for our lives: "All Scripture is God-breathed and is useful for teaching, rebuking, correcting, and training in righteousness, so that the servant of God may be thoroughly equipped for every good work." 2 Timothy 3:16–17 (NIV)

Additional Reading: 2 Timothy 3:14–17

FRIDAY

The gospel brings us together to share our lives. Paul told the church: "We loved you so much that we were delighted to share with you not only the gospel of God but our lives as well, because you had become so dear to us." 1 Thessalonians 2:8 (NIV)

Additional Reading: 1 Thessalonians 2:1–8

Open Intercession or Daily Intercession
For daily intercessions see Appendix F.

Prayer for the Week

God our Father, let the Spirit you sent to the early church continue to work in the world through the hearts of all who believe. We ask this through our Lord Jesus Christ, your Son, who lives and reigns with you and the Holy Spirit, one God, forever and ever. Amen. —*Based on a prayer of the Tessera Catena Legionis*

Song for the Season ✠
Sing a song of your choice.

THE FIFTH WEEK OF THE TIME OF THE KINGDOM

The Lighting of the Candle
The leader prays as a participant lights the candle.

LEADER   Let us pray. Spirit of God, come and empower your church. May we be a shining light, a city on a hill, dispelling darkness wherever we go.

Meditation or Silence ✠
After a moment of silence or a physical expression of prayer, the leader continues.

LEADER   Holy Spirit, you fill us, your children, with great joy.

Psalm

MONDAY • Psalm 105:1–6   **TUESDAY** • Psalm 105:7–15
WEDNESDAY • Psalm 105:16–22
THURSDAY • Psalm 105:23–38   **FRIDAY** • Psalm 105:39–45

Song for the Season ✠

Sing a song of your choice.

Short Verse

READER   The apostle John wrote: "See what kind of love the Father has given to us, that we should be called children of God; and so we are. The reason why the world does not know us is that it did not know him." 1 John 3:1

Short Prayer

READER   Spirit, teach us to receive the kingdom of God as a child.

Scripture Reading

EVERYONE   Father, open our eyes that we might see the wonders of your truth.

MONDAY

The apostle Paul wrote: "May the God of hope fill you with all joy and peace in believing, so that by the power of the Holy Spirit you may abound in hope." Romans 15:13

Additional Reading: Romans 15:1–7, 13

TUESDAY

We are sons and daughters of the Great King: "So you are no longer a slave, but a son, and if a son, then an heir through God." Galatians 4:7

Additional Reading: Galatians 4:4–7

WEDNESDAY

We are not servants, but dearly loved children: "To all who did receive him, who believed in his name, he gave the right to become children of God." John 1:12

Additional Reading: John 1:9–12

THURSDAY

His fatherly love runs deep: "See what kind of love the Father has given to us, that we should be called children of God; and so we are." I John 3:1

Additional Reading: 1 John 3:1–3, 18

FRIDAY

Love is the essence of the commandments: "Everyone who believes that Jesus is the Christ has been born of God, and everyone who loves the Father loves whoever has been born of him. By this we know that we love the children of God, when we love God and obey his commandments." I John 5:1–3

Additional Reading: 1 John 5:1–5

Open Intercession or Daily Intercession

For daily intercessions see Appendix F.

Prayer for the Week

Heavenly Father, look upon our humble community of believers who are a part of the church of your Son, Jesus Christ. Holy Spirit, help us be witnesses to his unfailing faithfulness where we live, demonstrating to the world that we are indeed his disciples through our love for each other. Let us indwell the reality of your presence in our homes, in our community, and in this city. Amen. —*A prayer of the Sequoia Community*

Song for the Season

Sing a song of your choice.

SIXTH WEEK OF THE TIME OF THE KINGDOM

The Lighting of the Candle

The leader prays as a participant lights the candle.

LEADER   Let us pray. Spirit of God, come and empower your church. May we be a shining light, a city on a hill, dispelling darkness wherever we go.

Meditation or Silence

After a moment of silence or a physical expression of prayer, the leader continues.

LEADER   Father, you guide us in the will of your love.

Psalm

MONDAY • Psalm 5:7–8   TUESDAY • Psalm 9:9–14   WEDNESDAY • Psalm 13:3–6
THURSDAY • Psalm 74:12–17   FRIDAY • Psalm 10:16–18

Song for the Season ✠

Sing a song of your choice.

Short Verse

READER   Paul wrote of Jesus, the head of the church: "And [God] put all things under [Jesus'] feet and gave him as head over all things to the church." Ephesians 1:22

Short Prayer

READER   Christ Jesus, encourage your people to enjoy the beauty of redemption.

Scripture Reading

EVERYONE   Father, open our eyes that we might see the wonders of your truth.

MONDAY

Jesus is the head of the church: "He is the head of the body, the church. He is the beginning, the firstborn from the dead, that in everything he might be preeminent. For in him all the fullness of God was pleased to dwell, and through him to reconcile to himself all things." Colossians 1:18–20

Additional Reading: Colossians 1:15–20

TUESDAY

Of Jesus Christ the Son, the psalmist writes: "Your throne, O God, is forever and ever, the scepter of uprightness is the scepter of your kingdom." Hebrews 1:8

Additional Reading: Hebrews 1:1–8; Psalm 45:6–7

WEDNESDAY

In Christ, the head of the church, God has made known his mystery: "To unite all things in him, things in heaven and things on earth." Ephesians 1:10

Additional Reading: Ephesians 1:1–10

THURSDAY

Christ in his glory said to John: "I am the first and the last, and the living one. I died, and behold I am alive forevermore." Revelation 1:17–18

Additional Reading: Revelation 1:12–18

FRIDAY

Jesus humbled himself, and God the Father exalted him: "God has highly exalted him and bestowed on him the name that is above every name, so that at the name of Jesus every knee should bow, in heaven and on earth and under the earth, and every tongue confess that Jesus Christ is Lord, to the glory of God the Father." Philippians 2:9–11

Additional Reading: Philippians 2:1–11

Open Intercession or Daily Intercession
For daily intercessions see Appendix F.

Prayer for the Week
Lord Jesus Christ, eternal King, God and man, crucified for mankind, look upon me with mercy and hear my prayer, for I trust in you. Have mercy on me, for even though I am sinful, the depth of your compassion never ends. *Amen.*
—*Based on a prayer of St. Ambrose*

Song for the Season
Sing a song of your choice.

SEVENTH WEEK OF THE TIME OF THE KINGDOM

The Lighting of the Candle
The leader prays as a participant lights the candle.

LEADER   Let us pray. Spirit of God, come and empower your church. May we be a shining light, a city on a hill, dispelling darkness wherever we go.

Meditation or Silence
After a moment of silence or a physical expression of prayer, the leader continues.

LEADER   Jesus, you visit us in darkness and provide us with your light.

Psalm
MONDAY • Psalm 78:1–16   TUESDAY • Psalm 78:17–31   WEDNESDAY • Psalm 78:32–55
THURSDAY • Psalm 78:56–66   FRIDAY • Psalm 78:67–72

Song for the Season ✠

Sing a song of your choice.

Short Verse

READER   Jesus said to Thomas, "I am the way, and the truth, and the life. No one comes to the Father except through me." John 14:6

Short Prayer

READER   Jesus, rid us of our worries and replace them with the peace of childlike trust.

Scripture Reading

EVERYONE   Father, open our eyes that we might see the wonders of your truth.

MONDAY

Jesus said to them: "I am the bread of life; whoever comes to me shall not hunger, and whoever believes in me shall never thirst." John 6:35

Additional Reading: John 6:35–40

TUESDAY

Jesus said: "I am the light of the world. Whoever follows me will not walk in darkness, but will have the light of life." John 8:12

Additional Reading: John 8:12–18

WEDNESDAY

Jesus said: "I am the resurrection and the life. Whoever believes in me, though he die, yet shall he live." John 11:25

Additional Reading: John 11:17–27

THURSDAY

Jesus taught us saying: "I am the good shepherd. The good shepherd lays down his life for the sheep." John 10:11

Additional Reading: John 10:1–14

FRIDAY

Jesus taught his disciples: "I am the vine; you are the branches. Whoever abides in me and I in him, he it is that bears much fruit, for apart from me you can do nothing." John 15:5

Additional Reading: John 15:1–5

182

Open Intercession or Daily Intercession
For daily intercessions see Appendix F.

Prayer for the Week

O God, who for our redemption gave your only-begotten Son to the death of the cross, and by his glorious resurrection delivered us from the power of our enemy: Grant us to die daily to sin, that we may evermore live with him in the joy of his resurrection; through Jesus Christ your Son our Lord, who lives and reigns with you and the Holy Spirit, one God, now and for ever. Amen. *—Based on a prayer of the Book of Common Prayer, 1979*

Song for the Season
Sing a song of your choice.

EIGHTH WEEK OF THE TIME OF THE KINGDOM

The Lighting of the Candle
The leader prays as a participant lights the candle.

LEADER Let us pray. Spirit of God, come and empower your church. May we be a shining light, a city on a hill, dispelling darkness wherever we go.

Meditation or Silence
After a moment of silence or a physical expression of prayer, the leader continues.

LEADER Jesus, you are our source of solace and of life.

Psalm
MONDAY • Psalm 95:1–7 TUESDAY • Psalm 23:1–6 WEDNESDAY • Psalm 40:1–3
THURSDAY • Psalm 79:8–9; 13 FRIDAY • Psalm 100:1–5

Song for the Season
Sing a song of your choice.

Short Verse
READER Jesus said: "I am the good shepherd; I know my sheep and my sheep know me—just as the Father knows me and I know the Father—and I lay down my life for the sheep." John 10:14–15 (NIV)

Short Prayer

READER Christ Jesus, you always come to us wherever we may be.

Scripture Reading

EVERYONE Father, open our eyes that we might see the wonders of your truth.

MONDAY

Jesus said: "My sheep hear my voice, and I know them, and they follow me." John 10:27

Additional Reading: John 10:22–30

TUESDAY

Peter writes: "Above all, keep loving one another earnestly, since love covers a multitude of sins." 1 Peter 4:8

Additional Reading: 1 Peter 4:7–11

WEDNESDAY

Jesus told the Pharisees: "The thief comes only to steal and kill and destroy. I came that they may have life and have it abundantly." John 10:10

Additional Reading: John 10:7–18

THURSDAY

With the best robe, a ring, sandals, and a great feast, the father welcomed the prodigal son back home: "'For this my son was dead, and is alive again; he was lost, and is found.' And they began to celebrate." Luke 15:24

Additional Reading: Luke 15:11–32

FRIDAY

God's love extends to those who are difficult to love: "God shows his love for us in that while we were still sinners, Christ died for us." Romans 5:8

Additional Reading: Romans 5:7–11

Open Intercession or Daily Intercession

For daily intercessions see Appendix F.

Prayer for the Week

God our Father, you never stop searching for all who have gone away from you. And by your forgiveness, you place on our finger the ring of the prodigal son, the ring of festival. Amen. *—Based on a prayer of the Taizé Community*

Song for the Season ✚

Sing a song of your choice.

Note: Depending on the calendar for the year, this week's liturgy may or may not be necessary. See Appendix C or the athomewithgod.org website for exact dates.

The Lighting of the Candle
The leader prays as a participant lights the candle.

LEADER   Let us pray. Spirit of God, come and empower your church. May we be a shining light, a city on a hill, dispelling darkness wherever we go.

Meditation or Silence ✚
After a moment of silence or a physical expression of prayer, the leader continues.

LEADER   Holy Spirit, we surrender to you in simplicity.

Psalm
MONDAY • Psalm 107:4–9   TUESDAY • Psalm 42:1–5
WEDNESDAY • Psalm 91:1–2; 11–16
THURSDAY • Psalm 88:1–2, 13–15   FRIDAY • Psalm 84:5–12

Song for the Season ✚
Sing a song of your choice.

Short Verse
READER   David wrote: "Even though I walk through the valley of the shadow of death, I will fear no evil." Psalm 23:4

Short Prayer
READER   Spirit of life, lead me and teach me to trust you—even in darkness.

Scripture Reading
EVERYONE   Father, open our eyes that we might see the wonders of your truth.

MONDAY
Though in pain, Job trusted God: "The Lord gave, and the Lord has taken away; blessed be the name of the Lord." Job 1:21
Additional Reading: Job 1:13–22

TUESDAY
Though the wilderness is difficult, is it there we learn to trust God: "Therefore, behold, I will allure her, and bring her into the wilderness, and speak tenderly to her." Hosea 2:14
Additional Reading: Hosea 2:14–15

WEDNESDAY

Jesus found the source of his ministry in the wilderness: "Jesus was led up by the Spirit into the wilderness to be tempted." Matthew 4:1

Additional Reading: Matthew 4:1–4

THURSDAY

Paul was content when he had much or when he had little: "I have learned in whatever situation I am to be content." Philippians 4:11

Additional Reading: Philippians 4:10–13

FRIDAY

Though they are difficult, trials and temptations strengthen our faith in God: "God is faithful, and he will not let you be tempted beyond your ability, but with the temptation he will also provide the way of escape, that you may be able to endure it." 1 Corinthians 10:13

Additional Reading: 1 Corinthians 10:1–13

Open Intercession or Daily Intercession
For daily intercessions see Appendix F.

Prayer for the Week

My Lord God, I have no idea where I am going. I do not see the road ahead of me. I cannot know for certain where it will end. Nor do I really know myself, and the fact that I think that I am following your will does not mean that I am actually doing so. But I believe that the desire to please you does in fact please you. And I hope I have that desire in all that I am doing. I hope that I will never do anything apart from that desire. And I know that if I do this you will lead me by the right road, though I may know nothing about it. Therefore will I trust you always though I may seem to be lost and in the shadow of death. I will not fear, for you are ever with me, and you will never leave me to face my perils alone. *Amen. —From* Thoughts in Solitude, *by Thomas Merton*

Song for the Season ✠
Sing a song of your choice.

The Celebration of New Life

The home gathering for Summer begins with a dinner. Where the liturgy for *The Celebration of Redemption* is ancient and rich, this liturgy is intended to be simple and accessible. The theme of this season is the presence of God living within his people, indwelling them by his Holy Spirit.

PREPARING FOR *The Celebration of New Life*

DECORATIONS ✠

Red tablecloths
Several red pillar candles
Numerous white votives and tea candles
Vibrantly colored flowers

FOOD ✠ This home gathering is designed to feel like an intimate feast or a banquet celebrating the nearness and intimacy of God and the unity that life in the Holy Spirit brings. The liturgy revolves around the food and the symbols on the table. Therefore, you may wish to place all the food on the table at the beginning of the meal, rather than bringing it out in courses. Also, the food should be served family style to encourage interaction and a spirit of community. Since food is a key component of the liturgy, elegant presentation may enhance the overall experience.

The foods of particular importance for this home gathering are these:

Sparkling water
Bread, honey, and cheese
Basket of various fruits and fresh vegetables
Olive oil and bread, symbol of the anointing of the Holy Spirit
Dates, figs, and/or grapes, symbols of God's freedom
Pomegranates
Entrée for the meal[60]
Cheesecake

MUSIC AND PRAYER ✚ The music and prayer time should be simple and intimate, a symbol of God's nearness during Pentecost.

READERS The host may select the readers prior to the meal.

LITURGY FOR
The Celebration of New Life

Introduction

LEADER Tonight, we celebrate the presence of God dwelling within us. Over thousands of years, God has unfolded a plan to dwell within his people. On the night of Pentecost, years of prophecy and anticipation were fulfilled when the Holy Spirit descended on the believers in Jerusalem.

Symbol of the Water

READER When you send your Spirit, all is created. You renew the face of the earth. May the glory of the Lord endure forever.

READER Holy Spirit, we thank you that you are among us. In the beginning, you lovingly hovered over the earth, overlooking every detail of creation.

EVERYONE Come, Holy Spirit.

The leader pours the sparkling water and the participants drink and converse.

Song for the Season ✚

Sing a song of your choice.

Symbol of Fire

As the participants continue to eat and converse, the leader gathers everyone's attention and reads.

LEADER Throughout the Scriptures, fire is a symbol of God's presence among his people.

READER[61] God appeared to Moses by speaking from a flaming bush. Though it was on fire, it was not consumed. Only that which is pure and of God can withstand the test of fire.

READER When God led his people out of Egypt, he promised to lead them to a land of promise. With a cloud by day and a pillar of fire by night, he guided his people and was faithful to them every step of the way.

READER When Elijah confronted the King and encountered his false prophets, God consumed the offering with fire, and the people recognized that the God of Abraham, Isaac, and Jacob alone was the true God. The people confessed, "The LORD, he is God."

LEADER Throughout the Old Covenant, God made his presence known to his people through fire. But there would come a day when the fire of his presence would burn within his people.

READER To Jeremiah God spoke and said: "This is the covenant I will make with my people when it is time. I will put my law in their minds and write it on their hearts. I will be their God, and they will be my people."[62]

READER God said, "I will put my Spirit within you, and you shall live, and I will place you in a land of promise. Then you shall know that I am the LORD. I have promised and I am faithful. My dwelling place will be within them and I will be their God and they will be my people."[63]

LEADER Tonight we celebrate God's fulfilled promise to dwell within his people. No longer would he need a building for a temple. His people would be his temple, the very presence of God.

READER When the day of Pentecost came, the believers all gathered in one place. Suddenly, a sound like the blowing of a violent wind came from heaven and filled the whole house where they were sitting. They saw what seemed to be tongues of fire that separated and came to rest on each of them. All of them were filled with the Holy Spirit.

LEADER Tonight we light the red candles as a symbol of God's presence with his people throughout history and a symbol of his presence with us now. Traditionally, the church has used the color red to remind us of the fire of the Spirit that descended at Pentecost. As we light the candles, we pray.

EVERYONE Come, Holy Spirit, fill the hearts of the faithful. Ignite us in the fire of your love.
Participants, preferably children if present, light the red pillar candles and the white votives.

Song for the Season ✠
Sing a song of your choice.

Bread, Honey, and Cheese
As the participants continue to eat and converse, the leader gathers everyone's attention and reads.

LEADER   God made a promise to Abraham that his descendants would become a great people and that God would guide his people to a land of blessing. Tonight we celebrate God's faithfulness and his leadership even through the wilderness.

READER   The Spirit's presence never leaves us. God's Spirit is always with us and is leading us to the land of promise, a land flowing with milk and honey. *The participants eat the honey, bread, and cheese and continue conversing.*

First Fruits and Fresh Vegetables ✠

As the participants continue to eat and converse, the leader gathers everyone's attention. The leader then picks up a basket or bundle of fruit and reads.

LEADER   The origin of this festival is rooted in the first fruits or the first harvest of the season. Tonight we are eating the sweet fruits and fresh vegetables of the season. These fruits represent a taste of what is to come.

READER   Though we often are wounded by the impact of the fallen world, we know that heaven yet touches earth. Our life in the Spirit allows us to see the world through God's eyes, and through this we receive a taste of his kingdom here on earth.

LEADER   By taking up our cross and following Jesus, we are graciously given a new life in his Holy Spirit. In him we exchange a life of selfish desire and begin to experience new life and the fruit of the Spirit.

EVERYONE   The fruit of the Spirit is love, joy, peace, patience, kindness, goodness, faithfulness, gentleness, self-control.

LEADER   Look on the table. We have fresh fruit, vegetables, and flowers representing the sweetness and the beauty of God's presence in our lives. Take time tonight to taste and see that the Lord is good. Enjoy the sweetness of a life lived in him.

The leader encourages the participants to enjoy the fruit and fresh garden vegetables.

Symbol of the Oil

As the participants continue to eat and converse, the leader gathers everyone's attention and reads.

LEADER   Most powerful Spirit: come down upon us and subdue us. From heaven where the ordinary is made glorious, and glory seems but ordinary, bathe us with the brilliance of your light like dew.[64]

READER   How beautiful and enjoyable it is when brothers and sisters dwell in peace. It is like rare anointing oil gently flowing down one's head, flowing down Aaron's beard, down the collar of his priestly robe. It is like the dew of Mount Hermon, flowing down the slopes of the great city. From that mountain, God pronounces his blessing upon your life forevermore.[65]

READER God is faithful and honors all his promises. And all his promises are complete in Jesus Christ. The Father has established us in Christ, the Anointed One, and has placed the seal of his promise on us, anointing us with the Holy Spirit, who now lives in our beings.

LEADER Tonight we eat the oil, reminding us of the Holy Spirit who lives within us. Because of the Spirit's presence, we live as brothers and sisters in peace. *Everyone takes the bread, dips into the oil, and eats.*

Symbol of the Dates, Figs, and/or Grapes ✚
As the participants continue to eat and converse, the leader gathers everyone's attention and reads.

LEADER Where the Spirit of the Lord is . . .

EVERYONE There is freedom.

READER For thousands of years, God's people have celebrated his presence and his voice on this holiday. Throughout many generations, the people of God have celebrated the gift of the Law. Today, we celebrate the gift of the Holy Spirit.

READER Moses received the Law from God on Mount Sinai, engraved in letters of stone.

LEADER And even though the Law came and condemned us, it was full of power and the presence of God. But the glory of the old covenant would fade.

READER But now we celebrate a new Law and a new covenant, where the glory of God does not fade. We do not come to Mount Sinai, the place where the Law was given, a place where we tremble with fear. We come to Mount Zion, the city of joyful celebration.[66]

LEADER Tonight we celebrate the freedom and the joy of the presence of God by the power of the Spirit. During King Solomon's reign the people celebrated the kingdom of God as a place of abundance, freedom, peace, and safety by eating dates, figs, and grapes.

READER King Solomon is known as the king of peace. During his reign, there was peace on all sides. The people of God lived in safety, each man under his own vine and fig tree.

LEADER Tonight we celebrate the kingdom of God, the place of God's peace. These fruits are symbols of the unfading glory of God's kingdom and our freedom and peace living in him.

The leader encourages the participants to eat the dates, figs, and grapes.

Song for the Season ⊕

Sing a song of your choice.

The Meal

LEADER   When the Holy Spirit came, the church was born. Those on whom the Spirit fell became a new people where the Law was no longer on tablets of stone, but in their hearts. No longer were the people of God limited to one nation. People from every nation became a part of a new people and a new covenant.

READER   People from every tribe and nation—women and men, older people and younger people, educated and uneducated, rich and poor—all of these became a part of God's new people, fulfilling the promises from thousands of years before.

READER   After the Spirit came, this newly formed people dedicated themselves to the apostles' teaching, to the fellowship, to the breaking of bread, and to prayer. They broke bread in their homes and ate together with glad and sincere hearts.

LEADER   Tonight we eat together as the people of God. Enjoy the meal and enjoy each other's company.

The leader encourages the participants to enjoy the conversation and meal as the evening continues. The liturgy pauses as the participants finish the meal.

Milk and Honey

LEADER   Historically, milk and honey have been used to celebrate the fulfillment of God's promises during this season. As we finish the evening, enjoy the dessert as a sign of God's faithfulness to you and his people.

The ancient tradition for this season is to eat dairy, which hearkens back to God's promise to lead his people to a land flowing with milk and honey. Therefore, cheesecake or cheese pastries have become traditional for this season.

Prayer and Worship

In the spirit of Acts 2, a simple open time of prayer and worship may be incorporated to highlight God's nearness through the presence of the Holy Spirit.

Preparing for the Season

✠ *This symbol denotes that additional resources or reminders may be found at the athomewithgod.org website.*

Preparing for the Season

*A*utumn is entirely within an ordinary season. We refer to this time this way:
THE TIME OF THE JOURNEY

The Time of the Journey

This season is the last of the year. Depending on the year, this portion of the season begins either the last weekend of August or the first weekend of September and extends to the end of November. For exact dates, see Appendix C or the athomewithgod.org website.

The theme of this season focuses on the journey of faith, where our final destination is the City of God. Beginning in Genesis 4 and spanning throughout the entirety of the Scriptures, the journey to the City of God is a central theme that explores the relationship between our earthly and heavenly citizenship. The journey requires faith in God to maintain an honest search for truth and beauty. Often, faith does not supply us with all the answers; rather, it provides us the lens to see and understand the complexities of our fallen existence and enables us to see the world through God's eyes. Our citizenship in the heavenly city should make us among the best citizens of our earthly cities.

This season also celebrates believers who have come before us and their faithfulness to pursue God, even in difficulty. *The Celebration of the Journey* is the climax of this season and celebrates the conclusion of God's redemptive plan when we enter the City of God.

Traditions for the Season

SPECIAL ACTIVITIES

DAYS OF BLESSING THE CITY   Families or home groups may wish to set aside special days during this season to bless the city or area where they live. This activity of blessing should not publicize the activity or the group, but rather should be humble and inconspicuous, full of generosity and love. The acts of blessing could be focused on a community or an area of poverty or one that is experiencing some form of difficulty. This activity could also reach out directly to those who are homeless or impoverished.

DAY OF REPENTANCE The Day of Repentance is based on the Hebrew holy day of fasting, the Day of Atonement (Yom Kippur). On this day, we lament the absence of the kingdom of God where we live. Families or home groups may gather on this day to have a somber time of prayer and repentance.

SPECIAL SYMBOLS FOR THE SEASON

Below is a list of signs and symbols that could be used for this season.

DARK RED OR BURNT ORANGE Dark red or burnt orange is the color for this season. This color comes from Rahab's scarlet rope, which was a sign to the Hebrew armies to spare her because she put her faith not in the walls of the city, but in the God of Israel.

TENTS Families or home groups may use tents—backyard tents or even living-room campouts—as a symbol during this season. Hebrews 11 reminds us that Abraham lived in tents, as did Isaac and Jacob, who were heirs with him of the same promise. They looked forward to the city with foundations, whose architect and builder is God.

VISIT TO A RIVER, LAKE, OR OTHER BODY OF WATER The river image is used in Psalm 46 and also in Revelation 21 when speaking of the City of God. Interestingly, the city of Jerusalem does not have a river running through it. Yet, a river running through a city is an image of God's sustaining and refreshing blessings. Families or home groups may plan an outing to a river or a lake.

An ancient tradition associated with the river during this time of year includes putting stones into our pockets and emptying them into the river, symbolic of casting off or putting aside anything that hinders us in our journey toward God's City.

WHITE STONES The symbol of the white stones is used in reference to the overcoming church in Revelation 2. These stones are connected to God's provision and to our need for strength to persevere, like the manna that God provided for his people in the wilderness. They may

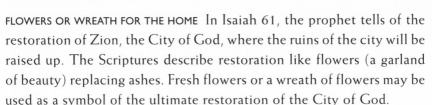

also symbolize a ticket of admission into the great festival in the new Jerusalem.

FLOWERS OR WREATH FOR THE HOME In Isaiah 61, the prophet tells of the restoration of Zion, the City of God, where the ruins of the city will be raised up. The Scriptures describe restoration like flowers (a garland of beauty) replacing ashes. Fresh flowers or a wreath of flowers may be used as a symbol of the ultimate restoration of the City of God.

HONEY BREAD OR GRANOLA The book of Exodus states that manna tasted like wafers that had been made with honey. Families may use honey bread or granola to symbolize the manna that God provided to the Israelites as they wandered through the desert en route to the land of promise.

DATES, GRAPES, AND FIGS Throughout the Scriptures, dates, grapes, and figs are used as symbols of the peace, justice, security, and prosperity of God's people. They also represent a return to a harmonious and fruitful relationship with God. Ultimate peace for the City of God is depicted as every man being able to sit under his date or fig tree eating the fruit of his tree.

HOME GATHERING

CELEBRATION OF THE JOURNEY   The final home gathering for the year draws from an ancient Hebrew festival that celebrates the final harvest of the season and, in turn, the final harvest of time. This gathering is designed to be celebratory and joyful and has a festival-like quality. Families and home groups may wish to set aside an entire day for this celebration. This home gathering is celebrated the weekend of the Columbus Day holiday, which is observed in the United States on the second Monday of October.

The Lighting of the Candle

LEADER The City of God does not need the sun or the moon to shine on it, for the glory of God gives it light. Jesus the Lamb is its lamp.

A participant lights the candle for the season.[68]

MEMBER We praise you, God, King of the Universe, for you have given us Jesus Christ our returning King, the ruler of the City of Peace.

EVERYONE We praise you, God, Creator and Redeemer.

LEADER We praise you, God, King of the Universe, for you have given us this day of rest. When you created the world, you rested on the seventh day. Your rest creates the possibility for our rest, for we choose to rest in you.

The Blessing

Families with children may want to insert a short prayer for each child here.

LEADER On this day of rest, Father, bless us with your peace and rest. May we remain faithful and enter the land of rest that you promised to our ancestors and created for those who believe.

Song of Blessing ✚

The Lord bless you and keep you;
The Lord make his face shine upon you.
The Lord be gracious to you.
And give you his peace, forever.

Telling the Redemptive Story

The questions below are designed for children. Older groups may omit them.

LEADER Where does our journey lead us?

CHILDREN To the City of God.

LEADER How will we reach the City of God?

CHILDREN By walking with God in faith.

LEADER Do we journey alone?

CHILDREN No, we walk with other believers, both past and present.

If the questions are omitted, the liturgy continues here.

LEADER   This season we celebrate the City of God, the City of Peace. Though the world vies for our allegiance, our citizenship is in God's City. May we be faithful overcomers in our journey to the City of God, and may we see the redemption of the City of Man through our obedience.

Readings for the Season ✠

FIRST WEEK OF THE TIME OF THE JOURNEY

Though the world was corrupt, God made a covenant with Noah: "I will establish my covenant with you, and you shall come into the ark, you, your sons, your wife, and your sons' wives with you." Genesis 6:18

Additional Reading: Genesis 6:11–12, 18–22
Weekday liturgies for this week are found on page 206.

SECOND WEEK OF THE TIME OF THE JOURNEY

Noah's life required great faith, as the world mocked him: "By faith Noah, being warned by God concerning events as yet unseen, in reverent fear constructed an ark for the saving of his household. . . . [He] became an heir of the righteousness that comes by faith." Hebrews 11:7

Additional Reading: Hebrews 11:4–7
Weekday liturgies for this week are found on page 208.

THIRD WEEK OF THE TIME OF THE JOURNEY

God told Abram: "Go from your country and your kindred and your father's house to the land that I will show you. And I will make of you a great nation, and I will bless you and make your name great, so that you will be a blessing." Genesis 12:1–2

Additional Reading: Genesis 12:1–3
Weekday liturgies for this week are found on page 210.

FOURTH WEEK OF THE TIME OF THE JOURNEY

Abraham trusted God, even when obedience seemed irrational: "He was tested, offered up Isaac, and he who had received the promises was in the act of offering up his only son, of whom it was said, 'Through Isaac shall your offspring be named.' He considered that God was able even to raise him from the dead." Hebrews 11:17–19

Additional Reading: Hebrews 11:17–22
Weekday liturgies for this week are found on page 212.

FIFTH WEEK OF THE TIME OF THE JOURNEY

By faith Moses resisted Pharaoh and remained obedient: "He considered the reproach of Christ greater wealth than the treasures of Egypt, for he was looking to the reward. By faith he left Egypt, not being afraid of the anger of the king, for he endured as seeing him who is invisible. By faith he kept the Passover and sprinkled the blood, so that the Destroyer of the firstborn might not touch them." Hebrews 11:26–28

Additional Reading: Hebrews 11:23–28
Weekday liturgies for this week are found on page 214.

SIXTH WEEK OF THE TIME OF THE JOURNEY

The journey of God's people begins in faith: "By faith the people crossed the Red Sea as on dry land, but the Egyptians, when they attempted to do the same, were drowned." Hebrews 11:29

Additional Reading: Hebrews 11:29–31; Exodus 15:1–18
Weekday liturgies for this week are found on page 216.

SEVENTH WEEK OF THE TIME OF THE JOURNEY

By faith Jericho fell and Rahab became the unlikely heroine: "By faith the walls of Jericho fell, after the people had marched around them for seven days." Hebrews 11:30 (NIV)

Additional Reading: Hebrews 11:30–31; Joshua 2:8–21
Weekday liturgies for this week are found on page 218.

EIGHTH WEEK OF THE JOURNEY

Our ancestors have endured much and shown great faith throughout all generations: "Therefore, since we are surrounded by so great a cloud of witnesses, let us also lay aside every weight, and sin which clings so closely, and let us run with endurance the race that is set before us, looking to Jesus, the founder and perfecter of our faith." Hebrews 12:1–2

Additional Reading: Hebrews 11:1–3
Weekday liturgies for this week are found on page 220.

NINTH WEEK OF THE TIME OF THE JOURNEY

The Lord spoke to his people and told them to go into the city of Babylon, build houses, plant gardens, and pray for the peace and prosperity of the city: "'For I know the plans I have for you,' declares the LORD, 'plans to prosper you and not to harm you, plans to give you hope and a future.'" Jeremiah 29:11 (NIV)

Additional Reading: Jeremiah 29:4–14
Weekday liturgies for this week are found on page 222.

TENTH WEEK OF THE TIME OF THE JOURNEY

The Anointed One will preach good news to the poor and bring restoration to Zion: "They will rebuild the ancient ruins and restore the places long devastated; they will renew the ruined cities that have been devastated for generations." Isaiah 61:4 (NIV)

Additional Reading: Isaiah 61:1–4
Weekday liturgies for this week are found on page 224.

ELEVENTH WEEK OF THE TIME OF THE JOURNEY

When the kingdom of God is made complete, everything will be at peace: "On that day there shall be no light, cold, or frost. And there shall be a unique day, which is known to the LORD, neither day nor night, but at evening time there shall be light. On that day living waters shall flow out from Jerusalem, half of them to the eastern sea and half of them to the western sea. It shall continue in summer as in winter. And the LORD will be king over all the earth. On that day the LORD will be one and his name one." Zechariah 14:6–9

Additional Reading: Zechariah 14:6–9; 16–21
Weekday liturgies for this week are found on page 226.

TWELFTH WEEK OF THE TIME OF THE JOURNEY

The apostle John wrote: "Then I saw a new heaven and a new earth, for the first heaven and the first earth had passed away, and the sea was no more. And I saw the holy city, new Jerusalem, coming down out of heaven from God, prepared as a bride adorned for her husband." Revelation 21:1–2

Additional Reading: Revelation 21:1–11
Weekday liturgies for this week are found on page 228.

FINAL WEEK OF THE LITURGICAL YEAR

The commandment for all generations is this: "Hear, O Israel: The LORD our God, the LORD is one. You shall love the LORD your God with all your heart and with all your soul and with all your might." Deuteronomy 6:4–5

Additional Reading: Deuteronomy 6:4–7
Weekday liturgies for this week are found on page 230.

ADDITIONAL Over dinner, older groups may want to engage in creative, explorative discussion of the Scriptures, in the ancient tradition of Midrash. See Appendix E.

Blessing the Cup

LEADER We praise you, God, King of the Universe, for you have given us the fruit of the vine. Father, we look forward to drinking wine with you and all the saints at the great wedding banquet of the Lamb.

The leader pours the wine or juice and passes the cup so everyone drinks.

Blessing the Bread and Oil

LEADER   We praise you, God, King of the Universe, for you give us bread from the earth. Jesus, we remember your words that your banquet table welcomes the poor. "Blessed is everyone who eats bread in the kingdom of God, who is invited to the wedding dinner of the Lamb."

LEADER   We also praise you, God, King of the Universe, for you give us this oil. Spirit, we have heard your counsel to the church. Renew our first love.

EVERYONE   We celebrate the birth, life, death, resurrection, ascension, and return of our King, Jesus Christ.

Everyone takes the bread, dips into the oil, and eats.

LEADER   Together we pray.

EVERYONE   Come, Lord Jesus, come.

Song of Celebration ✠
Sing a song of your choice.

The Peace of Sabbath

LEADER   The peace of Christ be with you.

EVERYONE   And also with you.

All pass the peace of Christ.

THE CLOSING OF SABBATH FOR THE TIME OF THE JOURNEY

The Greeting

LEADER   The Lord be with you.

EVERYONE   And also with you.

LEADER   When we are together, the Christ in me sees the Christ in you. Wherever we go, whatever we do, the ground we walk together is holy ground.

The Lighting of the Two Candles

The questions below are designed for children. Older groups may omit them.

LEADER   We part from the Sabbath ceremoniously, just as we welcomed it. This evening, we tell the conclusion of God's redemptive plan and celebrate our hope in its completion.

LEADER   What do the two candles symbolize?

CHILDREN   The City of God and the City of Man.

LEADER   How do we live as citizens of the City of God while we live in the City of Man?

CHILDREN   We pray and work for the peace of the city where we live.

If the questions are omitted, the liturgy continues here.

LEADER   God has sent his Spirit that his people might live the City of God here on earth. The Spirit and the Bride, which is the City of God, say: "Come, let all who are thirsty come take the free gift of the water of life." *Optional: For this season, stemmed glasses of water may be added to the liturgy.*

LEADER   We praise you, God, King of the Universe, who created light. Lamb of God, you are the light of the City of God and the light of this house. Illumine us with your presence. *Amen.*

One of the participants lights the two candles.

Song for the Season ✠

Sing a song of your choice.

The Cup of Blessing

The leader lifts the cup for all to see.

LEADER   We lift up the cup of salvation.

EVERYONE   For salvation belongs to our God.

LEADER   Father, your blessing be upon us now and forever.

The leader places the cup in a dish.

LEADER   We praise you, God, King of the Universe, for you have given us the fruit of the vine and you generously pour out your blessing on us.

EVERYONE   Fill our cups to overflowing.

LEADER   Jesus said that he will not taste wine again until he tastes the cup of restoration at the great wedding celebration of the Lamb. We look forward to celebrating the restoration of the City of God with a cup of wine with our Savior.

A participant places the cup in a dish and fills the cup until it overflows, then pours the remaining wine or juice into a cup for each member.

Short Prayer for the Week

LEADER   Though we know the truth of God's redemptive story, we often forget God. We become so accustomed to the world around us that we often blend in without thinking. These short prayers reconnect our spirits back to God's Spirit, asking him to tune our ears and refocus our attention as we journey to the City of God.

FIRST WEEK OF THE TIME OF THE JOURNEY
Father, kindle in us the faith of our ancestors.

SECOND WEEK OF THE TIME OF THE JOURNEY
Holy Spirit, give us joy in this journey.

THIRD WEEK OF THE TIME OF THE JOURNEY
King Jesus, direct our lives toward the Great City.

FOURTH WEEK OF THE TIME OF THE JOURNEY
Holy Spirit, remind us of our true identity and citizenship.

FIFTH WEEK OF THE TIME OF THE JOURNEY
Jesus, we believe. Help our unbelief.

SIXTH WEEK OF THE TIME OF THE JOURNEY
Father, you provide for us each step of our journey.

SEVENTH WEEK OF THE TIME OF THE JOURNEY
Holy Spirit, teach us to share our resources more freely.

EIGHTH WEEK OF THE TIME OF THE JOURNEY
Father, lead us into a sense of wonder at the beauty of your creation.

NINTH WEEK OF THE TIME OF THE JOURNEY
Spirit, give us the strength to endure and overcome.

TENTH WEEK OF THE TIME OF THE JOURNEY
Faithful One, enable us to remain always faithful to you.

ELEVENTH WEEK OF THE TIME OF THE JOURNEY
Awaken in us a desire for your peace and justice.

TWELFTH WEEK OF THE TIME OF THE JOURNEY
Holy Spirit, prepare our hearts and minds for your return.

FINAL WEEK OF THE LITURGICAL YEAR
Father, bless us as we journey together.

Conclusion of the Day of Rest

LEADER We now depart from our day of rest. Tomorrow we must return to work. One day, however, there will be no more work and we will have our final rest in the City of God. Until then, may we press on and overcome by living lives of peace, rooted in God's ways. *Amen.*

MEMBER God will prepare a feast with the best food and the greatest of aged wines, and his kingdom will have no end.

LEADER What do you think the great banquet will look like? What do you think we will eat? What will the music be like?

The participants imagine the great banquet.

A participant lights the incense and wafts it through the room.

LEADER We praise you, God, King of the Universe, for you have given us our memories, our desires, and our senses. With great joy we remember the sweetness of this day of rest and anticipate the day of rest to come.

The Lighting of the Candle

The leader prays as a participant lights the candle.[70]

LEADER Let us pray. Faithful God, you illumine the path of your people through the mystery of faith. Remind us of our journey to the Great City of God.

Meditation or Silence[71] ✟

After a moment of silence or a physical expression of prayer, the leader continues.

LEADER Holy Spirit, you renew us in your presence.

Psalms for the Week

MONDAY • Psalm 105:1–6   TUESDAY • Psalm 105:7–15
WEDNESDAY • Psalm 105:16–25
THURSDAY Psalm 105:26–38   FRIDAY • Psalm 105:39–45

Song for the Season ✟

Sing a song of your choice.

Short Verse

READER Wholehearted trust in God is the essence of our faith: "Without faith it is impossible to please [God], for whoever would draw near to God must believe that he exists and that he rewards those who seek him." Hebrews 11:6

Short Prayer

READER Father, kindle in us the faith of our ancestors.

Scripture Reading

EVERYONE Father, open our eyes that we might see the wonders of your truth.

MONDAY

Abel's faith pleased God: "By faith Abel offered to God a more acceptable sacrifice than Cain, through which he was commended as righteous, God commending him by accepting his gifts." Hebrews 11:4

Additional Reading: Genesis 4:1–9; Hebrews 11:4–5

TUESDAY

Trusting dependence on God is what holds all believers together and guides our lives: "The righteous shall live by his faith." Habakkuk 2:4

Additional Reading: Genesis 5:21–24; Hebrews 11:5–6

WEDNESDAY

Noah was a man of great faith who embraced God's rationality, as opposed to the world's: "And Noah did all that the LORD had commanded him." Genesis 7:5

Additional Reading: Genesis 7:1–24

THURSDAY

Noah's obedience required him to act unconventionally: "By faith Noah, being warned by God concerning events as yet unseen, in reverent fear constructed an ark for the saving of his household. By this he condemned the world and became an heir of the righteousness that comes by faith." Hebrews 11:7

Additional Reading: Genesis 8:1–22

FRIDAY

Noah gives us understanding of our own salvation and life: "God waited patiently in the days of Noah while the ark was being built. In it only a few people, eight in all, were saved through water, and this water symbolizes baptism that now saves you also." 1 Peter 3:20–21 (NIV)

Additional Reading: 1 Peter 3:18–22; Luke 17:20–36

Open Intercession or Daily Intercession
For daily intercessions see Appendix F.

Prayer for the Week

We acknowledge, O Lord, and give thanks that you have created us in your image, so that we might remember you, think of you, and love you. But this image is so worn away by the Fall, it is so obscured by our sins, that we cannot do what we were created to do unless you renew and reform us. We are not attempting, O Lord, to penetrate your loftiness, for we cannot begin to match our understanding with it, but we desire in some measure to understand your truth, which our hearts believe and love. For we do not seek to understand in order that we might believe, but we believe in order to understand. For this too we believe, that unless we believe, we will not understand. *Amen.* —*Based on a prayer of St. Anselm*

Song for the Season ✙
Sing a song of your choice.

The Lighting of the Candle

The leader prays as a participant lights the candle.

LEADER   Let us pray. Faithful God, you illumine the path of your people through the mystery of faith. Remind us of our journey to the great City of God.

Meditation or Silence ✚

After a moment of silence or a physical expression of prayer, the leader continues.

LEADER   Father, your love and your presence are transforming.

Psalm

MONDAY • Psalm 78:1–4   TUESDAY • Psalm 78:5–16   WEDNESDAY • Psalm 78:17–31
THURSDAY • Psalm 78:32–55   FRIDAY • Psalm 78:56–72

Song for the Season ✚

Sing a song of your choice.

Short Verse

READER   Our heritage begins in faith: "[Abraham] believed the LORD, and he counted it to him as righteousness." Genesis 15:6

Short Prayer

READER   Holy Spirit, give us joy in this journey.

Scripture Reading

EVERYONE   Father, open our eyes that we might see the wonders of your truth.

MONDAY

Though he did not know he was going, Abram left everything to go to a country where God was leading him: "For he was looking forward to the city that has foundations, whose designer and builder is God." Hebrews 11:10

Additional Reading: Genesis 12:1–9; Hebrews 11:8–10

TUESDAY

Though Abram's faith wavered, God was faithful: "Pharaoh gave men orders concerning him, and they sent him away with his wife and all that he had." Genesis 12:20

Additional Reading: Genesis 12:10–20

WEDNESDAY

Abram shared a table with Melchizedek, a shadow of Jesus Christ, the Great High Priest: "And Melchizedek king of Salem brought out bread and wine. (He was priest of God Most High.) And he blessed him." Genesis 14:18–19a

Additional Reading: Genesis 14:17–23

THURSDAY

Because we believe we are welcomed into the great heritage of faith: "Know then that it is those of faith who are the sons of Abraham." Galatians 3:7

Additional Reading: Genesis 15:1–6

FRIDAY

God warned Abram that his descendants would experience hardship and slavery, but he would honor his promise: "Know for certain that your offspring will be sojourners in a land that is not theirs and will be servants there, and they will be afflicted for four hundred years. But I will bring judgment on the nation that they serve, and afterward they shall come out with great possessions." Genesis 15:13–14

Additional Reading: Genesis 15:12–15

Open Intercession or Daily Intercession
For daily intercessions see Appendix F.

Prayer for the Week

Father in Heaven, what are we without you? All that we know—even though we may know great things—is but a chipped fragment if we do not know you. What is all our striving, could it ever encompass a world, but a half-finished work if we do not know you? You are the One who is the One Thing and who is all.

So may you give to the intellect, wisdom to comprehend that one thing; to the heart, sincerity to receive this understanding; to the will, purity that wills only one thing. In prosperity may you grant perseverance to will one thing; amid distractions, collectedness to will one thing; in suffering, patience to will one thing. *Amen.*

—*Based on a prayer of Søren Kierkegaard*

Song for the Season
Sing a song of your choice.

The Lighting of the Candle

The leader prays as a participant lights the candle.

LEADER Let us pray. Faithful God, you illumine the path of your people through the mystery of faith. Remind us of our journey to the great City of God.

Meditation or Silence ✠

After a moment of silence or a physical expression of prayer, the leader continues.

LEADER In the depths of our souls, Spirit, you provide a sense of wonder.

Psalm

MONDAY • Psalm 120   TUESDAY • Psalm 121   WEDNESDAY • Psalm 122
THURSDAY • Psalm 123   FRIDAY • Psalm 124

Song for the Season ✠

Sing a song of your choice.

Short Verse

READER Cain, cursed as a wanderer, built a city. Abraham, blessed by God, wandered to find a city designed by God: "For [Abraham] was looking forward to the city that has foundations, whose designer and builder is God." Hebrews 11:10

Short Prayer

READER King Jesus, direct our lives toward the Great City.

Scripture Reading

EVERYONE Father, open our eyes that we might see the wonders of your truth.

MONDAY

Abraham trusted God so deeply that even though he did not know how, he believed that Isaac would return with him: "God will provide for himself the lamb for a burnt offering, my son." Genesis 22:8

Additional Reading: Genesis 22:1–8

TUESDAY

Abraham was willing to offer up that which was most dear to him—he did not even withhold his son: "By faith Abraham, when he was tested, offered up Isaac, and he who had received the promises was in the act of offering up his only son." Hebrews 11:17

Additional Reading: Genesis 22:9–18; Hebrews 11:17–19

WEDNESDAY

The Lord blessed Abram in every way, and Isaac continued God's story in establishing God's people: "To your offspring I will give this land." Genesis 24:7

Additional Reading: Genesis 24:1–7

THURSDAY

Jacob was ambitious for God: "I will not let you go unless you bless me." Genesis 32:26

Additional Reading: Genesis 32:22–30; Hebrews 11:20–21

FRIDAY

Joseph was faithful. Despite difficult circumstances, he believed in God. He told his brothers: "You meant evil against me, but God meant it for good." Genesis 50:20

Additional Reading: Genesis 45:4–15, 50:15–21; Hebrews 11:22

Open Intercession or Daily Intercession
For daily intercessions see Appendix F.

Prayer for the Week

Great are you, O Lord, and exceedingly worthy of praise; your power is immense, and your wisdom beyond reckoning. And so we, who are a due part of your creation, long to praise you. We also carry our mortality about with us, carry the evidence of our sin and with it the proof that you thwart the proud. You arouse us so that praising you may bring us joy, because you have made us and drawn us to yourself, and our heart is unquiet until it rests in you. *Amen. —Based on a prayer of St. Augustine*

Song for the Season ✠
Sing a song of your choice.

The Lighting of the Candle

The leader prays as a participant lights the candle.

LEADER   Let us pray. Faithful God, you illumine the path of your people through the mystery of faith. Remind us of our journey to the Great City of God.

Meditation or Silence ✚

After a moment of silence or a physical expression of prayer, the leader continues.

LEADER   Jesus, you have placed in our hearts a longing for your kingdom.

Psalm

MONDAY • Psalm 125   TUESDAY • Psalm 126   WEDNESDAY • Psalm 127
THURSDAY • Psalm 128   FRIDAY • Psalm 129

Song for the Season ✚

Sing a song of your choice.

Short Verse

READER   The apostle Peter wrote: "I urge you as sojourners and exiles to abstain from the passions of the flesh, which wage war against your soul." I Peter 2:11

Short Prayer

READER   Holy Spirit, remind us of our true identity and citizenship.

Scripture Reading

EVERYONE   Father, open our eyes that we might see the wonders of your truth.

MONDAY

The faith of one household paved the way for Israel's salvation: "By faith Moses' parents hid him for three months after he was born, because they saw he was no ordinary child, and they were not afraid of the king's edict." Hebrews 11:23 (NIV)

Additional Reading: Exodus 2:1–10

TUESDAY

God is always faithful and never forgets his promises: "God heard their groaning, and God remembered his covenant with Abraham, with Isaac, and with Jacob." Exodus 2:24

Additional Reading: Exodus 2:23–25

WEDNESDAY

The fire of the Spirit came upon the bush and God told Moses: "Take off your sandals, for the place where you are standing is holy ground." Exodus 3:5 (NIV)

Additional Reading: Exodus 3:1–17

THURSDAY

From the beginning God has desired to establish his people: "I will take you as my own people, and I will be your God. Then you will know that I am the LORD your God." Exodus 6:7 (NIV)

Additional Reading: Exodus 6:1–9

FRIDAY

Early in the heritage of his people, God promised a kingdom that would last forever. Moses praised God: "You will bring them in and plant them on your own mountain. . . . The LORD will reign forever and ever." Exodus 15:17–18

Additional Reading: Exodus 15:13–18

Open Intercession or Daily Intercession

For daily intercessions see Appendix F.

Prayer for the Week

Father, we pray that the eyes of our heart may be enlightened in order that we may know the hope to which you have called us, the riches of your glorious inheritance in the saints, and your incomparably great power for us who believe. Father, the power you have given us is the mighty strength which you exerted in Christ when you raised him from the dead and seated him at your right hand in the heavenly realms, far above all rule and authority, power and dominion, and every title that can be given, not only in the present age but also in the one to come. *Amen.*
—*Based on the text of Ephesians 1*

Song for the Season ⊕

Sing a song of your choice.

214

The Lighting of the Candle

The leader prays as a participant lights the candle.

LEADER   Let us pray. Faithful God, you illumine the path of your people through the mystery of faith. Remind us of our journey to the Great City of God.

Meditation or Silence ✚

After a moment of silence or a physical expression of prayer, the leader continues.

LEADER   Christ Jesus, you offer us the fullness of life.

Psalm

MONDAY • Psalm 130   **TUESDAY** • Psalm 131   **WEDNESDAY** • Psalm 132
THURSDAY • Psalm 133   **FRIDAY** • Psalm 134

Song for the Season ✚

Sing a song of your choice.

Short Verse

READER   Jesus said to the father of an afflicted child: "'All things are possible for one who believes.' Immediately the father of the child cried out and said, 'I believe; help my unbelief!'" Mark 9:23–24

Short Prayer

READER   Jesus, we believe. Help our unbelief.

Scripture Reading

EVERYONE   Father, open our eyes that we might see the wonders of your truth.

MONDAY

Joshua believed God and told the people: "The LORD will do wonders among you." Joshua 3:5

Additional Reading: Joshua 3:7–17

TUESDAY

God told Joshua to use the small stones as symbols to recount God's word to the people's children: "Tell them the flow of the Jordan was cut off before the ark of the covenant of the Lord." Joshua 4:7 (NIV)

Additional Reading: Joshua 4:1–7

WEDNESDAY

Rahab had no claim of righteousness through heritage or morality, but God counted her as righteous because of her faith. "Joshua spared Rahab the prostitute, with her family and all who belonged to her." Joshua 6:25 (NIV)

Additional Reading: Joshua 5:13–15, 6:15–23; Hebrews 11:30–31

THURSDAY

Another woman outside of the nation that God had chosen exhibited great faith, and like Rahab, Ruth became a grandmother of the Messiah. Ruth told Naomi: "Your people shall be my people, and your God my God." Ruth 1:16

Additional Reading: Ruth 1:15–18, 4:9–17

FRIDAY

A Roman soldier with no roots in the faith showed greater faith than most in Israel. The soldier told Jesus: "I am not worthy to have you come under my roof. . . . But say the word, and let my servant be healed." Luke 7:6–7

Additional Reading: Luke 7:1–10

Open Intercession or Daily Intercession
For daily intercessions see Appendix F.

Prayer for the Week

Hold us fast, O Lord of Hosts, that we might not fall from you. Grant us thankful and obedient hearts that we might increase daily in the love, knowledge, and fear of you. Increase our faith and help our unbelief that we, being provided for and relieved in all our need by your fatherly care and provision, may be empowered to live godly lives to the praise of you, our Father in heaven, through Jesus Christ our Savior. Amen. *—Based on a prayer by Bishop James Pilkington*

Song for the Season ✠
Sing a song of your choice.

The Lighting of the Candle

The leader prays as a participant lights the candle.

LEADER   Let us pray. Faithful God, you illumine the path of your people through the mystery of faith. Remind us of our journey to the Great City of God.

Meditation or Silence ✛

After a moment of silence or a physical expression of prayer, the leader continues.

LEADER   God, only in you do our souls find rest.

Psalm

MONDAY • Psalm 113 and 114   **TUESDAY** • Psalm 115   **WEDNESDAY** • Psalm 116
THURSDAY • Psalm 117   **FRIDAY** • Psalm 118

Song for the Season ✛

Sing a song of your choice.

Short Verse

READER   Jesus said: "Man shall not live by bread alone, but by every word that comes from the mouth of God." Matthew 4:4

Short Prayer

READER   Father, you provide for us each step of our journey.

Scripture Reading

EVERYONE   Father, open our eyes that we might see the wonders of your truth.

MONDAY

Though the people grumbled, God provided for them every step of the way: "Behold, I am about to rain bread from heaven for you, and the people shall go out and gather a day's portion." Exodus 16:4

Additional Reading: Exodus 16:4–7

TUESDAY

After all God had done, the people still quarreled with Moses: "They tested the LORD by saying, 'Is the LORD among us or not?'" Exodus 17: 7

Additional Reading: Exodus 17:1–7

WEDNESDAY

Even though the people were stubborn, Moses interceded: "Now therefore, if I have found favor in your sight, please show me now your ways, that I may know you in order to find favor in your sight. Consider too that this nation is your people." Exodus 33:13

Additional Reading: Exodus 33:7–23

THURSDAY

The entire story of the Exodus led to this dramatic moment—when God moved from outside the camp to dwell in the midst of his people: "The glory of the Lord filled the tabernacle." Exodus 40:34

Additional Reading: Exodus 40:34–38

FRIDAY

The Feast of Tabernacles reminded the people of their journey with God through the desert. He provided for them every step of the way. God said: "You shall dwell in booths, . . . that your generations may know that I made the people of Israel dwell in booths when I brought them out of the land of Egypt: I am the Lord your God." Leviticus 23:42–43

Additional Reading: Deuteronomy 16:13–16

Open Intercession or Daily Intercession
For daily intercessions see Appendix F.

Prayer for the Week

Father, forgive us when we hold on to possessions or money rather than clinging to you in faith. We fear poverty, or hunger, or old age, or illness, or rejection. So often, we lay our hope on our material resources rather than upon you, our God, the Maker and Provider of the whole creation, even of the last and least of living things. *Amen. —Based on a prayer of St. Maximus the Confessor*

Song for the Season ✠
Sing a song of your choice.

The Lighting of the Candle

The leader prays as a participant lights the candle.

LEADER   Let us pray. Faithful God, you illumine the path of your people through the mystery of faith. Remind us of our journey to the Great City of God.

Meditation or Silence

After a moment of silence or a physical expression of prayer, the leader continues.

LEADER   Father, teach us to live in the simplicity of life in the Holy Spirit.

Psalm

MONDAY • Psalm 145:1–9 TUESDAY • Psalm 146 WEDNESDAY • Psalm 147
THURSDAY • Psalm 148 FRIDAY • Psalm 149 and 150

Song for the Season

Sing a song of your choice.

Short Verse

READER   John wrote of Jesus: "The Word became flesh and dwelt among us, and we have seen his glory, glory as of the only Son from the Father, full of grace and truth." John 1:14

Short Prayer

READER   Holy Spirit, teach us to share our resources freely.

Scripture Reading

EVERYONE   Father, open our eyes that we might see the wonders of your truth.

MONDAY

Solomon announced: "Now the LORD has fulfilled his promise that he made . . . and I have built the house for the name of the LORD, the God of Israel." 1 Kings 8:20

Additional Reading: 1 Kings 8:2–21

TUESDAY

At the dedication of the temple Solomon prayed: "The LORD our God be with us, as he was with our fathers. May he not leave us or forsake us." 1 Kings 8:57

Additional Reading: 1 Kings 8:54–66

WEDNESDAY

At the Feast of Tabernacles, Jesus announced that he was the perfect expression of the presence of God. "If anyone thirsts, let him come to me and drink." John 7:37

Additional Reading: John 7:37–44

THURSDAY

When God's plan is complete, all nations will gather to celebrate the Feast of Tabernacles. And on that day, as Zechariah prophesied, "The LORD will be king over all the earth." Zechariah 14:9

Additional Reading: Zechariah 14:6–9

FRIDAY

At the final Feast of Tabernacles the multitude from every nation will praise Jesus, saying: "Salvation belongs to our God who sits on the throne, and to the Lamb!" Revelation 7:10

Additional Reading: Revelation 7:9–17

Open Intercession or Daily Intercession
For daily intercessions see Appendix F.

Prayer for the Week

Lord our God, when we are afraid, do not permit us to doubt. When we are disappointed, let us not become bitter. When we have fallen, do not leave us lying down. When we have come to the end of our understanding and our powers, do not leave us to die. No, let us then feel your nearness and your love, which you have promised to those whose hearts are humble and broken, and who fear your Word. Amen. —*Based on a prayer of Karl Barth*

Song for the Season
Sing a song of your choice.

The Lighting of the Candle

The leader prays as a participant lights the candle.

LEADER   Let us pray. Faithful God, you illumine the path of your people through the mystery of faith. Remind us of our journey to the Great City of God.

Meditation or Silence ✠

After a moment of silence or a physical expression of prayer, the leader continues.

LEADER   Jesus, teach our hearts to listen to your voice.

Psalm

MONDAY • Psalm 46:1–7   **TUESDAY** • Psalm 46:8–11   **WEDNESDAY** • Psalm 47:1–9
THURSDAY • Psalm 48:1–8   **FRIDAY** • Psalm 48:9–14

Song for the Season ✠

Sing a song of your choice.

Short Verse

READER   Throughout all of the Scriptures we are reminded: "The righteous shall live by his faith." Habakkuk 2:4

Short Prayer

READER   Father, give us a sense of wonder at the beauty of creation.

Scripture Reading

EVERYONE   Father, open our eyes that we might see the wonders of your truth.

MONDAY

Though the opposing army was vast, God reminded the king: "The battle is not yours but God's." 2 Chronicles 20:15

Additional Reading: 2 Chronicles 20:15–26

TUESDAY

Though he was small, his faith was great. David told his opponent: "I come to you in the name of the LORD of hosts." 1 Samuel 17:45

Additional Reading: 1 Samuel 17:41–50

WEDNESDAY

The evil king was astonished because he cast three men into the fire: "But I see four men unbound, walking in the midst of the fire, and they are not hurt; and the appearance of the fourth is like a son of the gods." Daniel 3:25

Additional Reading: Daniel 3:8–30

THURSDAY

God and Elijah wanted to make sure that everyone knew it was God who was the only God: "'O Lord, God of Abraham, Isaac, and Israel, let it be known this day that you are God.' Then the fire of the Lord fell." 1 Kings 18:36

Additional Reading: 1 Kings 18:25–39

FRIDAY

When Daniel was lifted from the den, no wound was found on him because he had trusted in his God. King Darius responded to God's protection of Daniel, saying: "He is the living God, enduring forever; his kingdom shall never be destroyed, and his dominion shall be to the end." Daniel 6:26

Additional Reading: Daniel 6:6–27; Hebrews 11:32–34

Open Intercession or Daily Intercession
For daily intercessions see Appendix F.

Prayer for the Week

O Lord, grant us faith—the faith that removes the mask of the world and manifests God in all things; the faith that shows us Christ where our eyes only see a poor person; the faith that shows us a Savior where we feel only pain. O Lord, grant us the faith that inspires us to undertake everything that God wants without hesitation, without shame, without fear, and without ever retreating; the faith that knows how to go through life with calm, peace, and profound joy and that makes the soul completely indifferent to everything that is not you, O Jesus Christ, our Lord. *Amen.*
—*Based on a prayer of Charles de Foucauld*

Song for the Season ✠
Sing a song of your choice.

The Lighting of the Candle

The leader prays as a participant lights the candle.

LEADER Let us pray. Faithful God, you illumine the path of your people through the mystery of faith. Remind us of our journey to the Great City of God.

Meditation or Silence ☩

After a moment of silence or a physical expression of prayer, the leader continues.

LEADER Jesus, teach us to root our lives in your trust.

Psalm

MONDAY • Psalm 2:1–8 **TUESDAY** • Psalm 9:7–14 **WEDNESDAY** • Psalm 14:1–2, 7
THURSDAY • Psalm 50:1–6 **FRIDAY** • Psalm 51:15–19

Song for the Season ☩

Sing a song of your choice.

Short Verse

READER Our heritage is rich: "Therefore, since we are surrounded by so great a cloud of witnesses, let us also lay aside every weight, and sin which clings so closely, and let us run with endurance the race that is set before us, looking to Jesus, the founder and perfecter of our faith." Hebrews 12:1–2

Short Prayer

READER Spirit, give us strength to endure and overcome.

Scripture Reading

EVERYONE Father, open our eyes that we might see the wonders of your truth.

MONDAY

Even though she was not from Israel, the woman believed and received back her son from the dead: "And the woman said to Elijah, 'Now I know that you are a man of God, and that the word of the LORD in your mouth is truth.'" 1 Kings 17:24

Additional Reading: 1 Kings 17:8–24; Hebrews 11:35

TUESDAY

Within the sorrow of captivity, Jeremiah remembered God's faithfulness: "Because of the LORD's great love we are not consumed, for his compassions never fail. They are new every morning; great is your faithfulness." Lamentations 3:23 (NIV)

Additional Reading: Lamentations 3:1–24

WEDNESDAY

The writer of Hebrews reminds us that many of the faithful, such as the prophet Isaiah, were persecuted for their faith: "They were stoned, they were sawn in two, they were killed with the sword." Hebrews 11:37

Additional Reading: Isaiah 40:1–31; Hebrews 11:36–37

THURSDAY

Some were called to radical lives: "They went about in skins of sheep and goats, destitute, afflicted, mistreated—of whom the world was not worthy—wandering about in deserts and mountains, and in dens and caves of the earth." Hebrews 11:37–38

Additional Reading: Matthew 14:1–12

FRIDAY

Paul was resilient: "The crowds . . . stoned Paul and dragged him out of the city, supposing that he was dead. But when the disciples gathered about him, he rose up and entered the city." Acts 14:19–20

Additional Reading: Acts 14:8–22

Open Intercession or Daily Intercession

For daily intercessions see Appendix F.

Prayer for the Week

O Christ, those holy ones, the heirs of the eternal country, one and all with utter joy proclaim in a most worthy strain: have mercy on us. O King of kings, blessed redeemer; upon those who have been ransomed from the power of death, by your own blood, ever have mercy. We your people, throughout all ages, stand in your presence and cry, "Holy, Holy, Holy." Lord, have mercy on us. Amen. —*Based on a prayer of St. Dunstan, Archbishop of Canterbury*

Song for the Season

Sing a song of your choice.

224

The Lighting of the Candle

The leader prays as a participant lights the candle.

LEADER   Let us pray. Faithful God, you illumine the path of your people through the mystery of faith. Remind us of our journey to the Great City of God.

Meditation or Silence ✚

After a moment of silence or a physical expression of prayer, the leader continues.

LEADER   Holy Spirit, you remind us of the joy of our forgiveness.

Psalm

MONDAY • Psalm 53:1–2, 6 **TUESDAY** • Psalm 65:1–13
WEDNESDAY • Psalm 69:29–36
THURSDAY • Psalm 74:12–16 **FRIDAY** • Psalm 84:1–12

Song for the Season ✚

Sing a song of your choice.

Short Verse

READER   God encouraged his people: "I know the plans I have for you, declares the LORD, plans for welfare and not for evil, to give you a future and a hope. Then you will call upon me and come and pray to me, and I will hear you. You will seek me and find me, when you seek me with all your heart." Jeremiah 29:11–13

Short Prayer

READER   Faithful One, enable us to remain always faithful to you.

Scripture Reading

EVERYONE   Father, open our eyes that we might see the wonders of your truth.

MONDAY

God had compassion on the great city of Nineveh: "Go to the great city of Nineveh and proclaim to it the message I give you." Jonah 3:2 (NIV)

Additional Reading: Jonah 3:1–10, 4:1–11

TUESDAY

Zion is the city of celebration, the city of peace: "Look upon Zion, the city of our festivals; your eyes will see Jerusalem, a peaceful abode." Isaiah 33:20 (NIV)

Additional Reading: Isaiah 33:17–22

WEDNESDAY

The redeemed will enter Zion's gates singing: "The ransomed of the LORD will return. They will enter Zion with singing; everlasting joy will crown their heads. Gladness and joy will overtake them, and sorrow and sighing will flee away." Isaiah 51:11 (NIV)

Additional Reading: Isaiah 51:1–11

THURSDAY

"How beautiful on the mountains are the feet of those who bring good news, who proclaim peace, who bring good tidings, who proclaim salvation, who say to Zion, 'Your God reigns!'" Isaiah 52:7 (NIV)

Additional Reading: Isaiah 52:7–12

FRIDAY

God says of the Great City of Peace: "Arise, shine, for your light has come, and the glory of the LORD rises upon you . . . all who despise you will bow down at your feet and call you the City of the LORD." Isaiah 60:1, 14a (NIV)

Additional Reading: Isaiah 60:1–3, 10–14

Open Intercession or Daily Intercession

For daily intercessions see Appendix F.

Prayer for the Week

Grant, Almighty God, that as we live in this mortal body, yes, and nourish through sin a thousand deaths within us; O grant that we, by faith, will direct our eyes toward heaven, and to that incomprehensible power, which is to be fully revealed at the last day by you, Jesus Christ our Lord. In the midst of death may we find our hope in you, our Redeemer, and enjoy that redemption which you completed when you rose from the dead, and not doubt that the fruit that he then brought forth by his Spirit will come also to us when Christ himself shall come to judge the world; may we be partakers of that glory which by his death he has procured for us. Amen. —*Based on a prayer by John Calvin*

Song for the Season

Sing a song of your choice.

226

The Lighting of the Candle

The leader prays as a participant lights the candle.

LEADER Let us pray. Faithful God, you illumine the path of your people through the mystery of faith. Remind us of our journey to the Great City of God.

Meditation or Silence

After a moment of silence or a physical expression of prayer, the leader continues.

LEADER Holy Spirit, you awaken in us a sense of your presence.

Psalm

MONDAY • Psalm 87:1–7 **TUESDAY** • Psalm 97:1–12 **WEDNESDAY** • Psalm 99:1–9
THURSDAY • Psalm 102:12–22 **FRIDAY** • Psalm 110:1–7

Song for the Season

Sing a song of your choice.

Short Verse

READER God promised to restore all things in the City of God: "They shall call you the City of the LORD, the Zion of the Holy One of Israel." Isaiah 60:14b

Short Prayer

READER Awaken in me a desire for your peace and justice.

Scripture Reading

EVERYONE Father, open our eyes that we might see the wonders of your truth.

MONDAY

Joel reminded the people of the Great City that God is generous: "Be glad, O people of Zion, rejoice in the LORD your God, for he has given you the autumn rains in righteousness. He sends you abundant showers, both autumn and spring rains, as before." Joel 2:23 (NIV)

Additional Reading: Joel 2:23–27

TUESDAY

The promise began with one man, Abraham, and ends with a countless multitude: "I looked and there before me was a great multitude that no one could count, from every nation, tribe, people and language, standing before the throne and in front of the Lamb." Revelation 7:9 (NIV)

Additional Reading: Revelation 7:9–12

WEDNESDAY

God, the Redeemer, has promised to restore all things: "I am the LORD, who made all things, who alone stretched out the heavens, who spread out the earth by myself . . . saying of Jerusalem, 'She shall be built,' and of the temple, 'Your foundation shall be laid.'" Isaiah 44:24, 28b

Additional Reading: Isaiah 44:21–28

THURSDAY

The river brings gladness and beauty to the City of God: "There is a river whose streams make glad the city of God, the holy place where the Most High dwells." Psalm 46:4 (NIV)

Additional Reading: Psalm 46:1–7, Revelation 22:1–2

FRIDAY

The progress of redemption reaches from the Garden to the City: "I saw the Holy City, the new Jerusalem, coming down out of heaven from God, prepared as a bride beautifully dressed for her husband." Revelation 21:2 (NIV)

Additional Reading: Revelation 21:1–4

Open Intercession or Daily Intercession
For daily intercessions see Appendix F.

Prayer for the Week

Jesus, we repent. For we have built well and yet have forgotten the Cornerstone. We talk of right relations among men, but not of relations of men to God. You have told us that our citizenship is in heaven, the model and type for our citizenship upon earth. We build in vain unless the Lord builds with us. Loving Architect, we chose to build only with you. *Amen. —Inspired by "Choruses from* The Rock," *by T.S. Eliot*

Song for the Season ✠
Sing a song of your choice.

The Lighting of the Candle

The leader prays as a participant lights the candle.

LEADER   Let us pray. Faithful God, you illumine the path of your people through the mystery of faith. Remind us of our journey to the Great City of God.

Meditation or Silence

After a moment of silence or a physical expression of prayer, the leader continues.

LEADER   Spirit of Truth, you remind us of our home in God's City.

Psalm

MONDAY • Psalm 22:1–10   **TUESDAY** • Psalm 37:1–7   **WEDNESDAY** • Psalm 62:5–8
THURSDAY • Psalm 95:1–7   **FRIDAY** • Psalm 39:6–13

Song for the Season

Sing a song of your choice.

Short Verse

READER   The Psalmist wrote: "Great is the LORD and greatly to be praised in the city of our God." Psalm 48:1

Short Prayer

READER   Holy Spirit, prepare our hearts and minds for your return.

Scripture Reading

EVERYONE   Father, open our eyes that we might see the wonders of your truth.

MONDAY

Isaiah prophesied: "As a bridegroom rejoices over his bride, so will your God rejoice over you." Isaiah 62:5 (NIV)

Additional Reading: Isaiah 62:1–5

TUESDAY

The great mystery of Christ and his Bride, the church, is expressed in the power of mutual submission: "Submit to one another out of reverence for Christ." Ephesians 5:21 (NIV)

Additional Reading: Ephesians 5:22–32

WEDNESDAY

The bridegroom is zealous for his bride. His love will not be stopped: "Place me like a seal over your heart, like a seal on your arm; for love is as strong as death, its jealousy unyielding as the grave. It burns like blazing fire, like a mighty flame." Song of Solomon 8:6 (NIV)

Additional Reading: Song of Solomon 8:3–7, 14

THURSDAY

Once his people were a deserted wife, but now her husband has redeemed her with love and compassion: "For your Maker is your husband—the LORD Almighty is his name—the Holy One of Israel is your Redeemer; he is called the God of all the earth." Isaiah 54:5 (NIV)

Additional Reading: Isaiah 54:4–5

FRIDAY

The wise bride stands ready, awaiting the return of her bridegroom: "Here's the bridegroom! Come out to meet him!" Matthew 25:6 (NIV)

Additional Reading: Matthew 25:1–13

Open Intercession or Daily Intercession
For daily intercessions see Appendix F.

Prayer for the Week

And I pray that you will lead me, a sinner, to the banquet where you, with your Son and Holy Spirit, are true and perfect light, total fulfillment, everlasting joy, gladness without end, and perfect happiness to your saints.

Grant this through Christ our Lord. *Amen.* —*Based on a prayer of St. Thomas Aquinas*

Song for the Season ✠
Sing a song of your choice.

The Lighting of the Candle

The leader prays as a participant lights the candle.

LEADER   Let us pray. Faithful God, you illumine the path of your people through the mystery of faith. Remind us of our journey to the Great City of God.

Meditation or Silence

After a moment of silence or a physical expression of prayer, the leader continues.

LEADER   Father, for all you have done and all you do, we are truly thankful.

Psalm

MONDAY • Psalm 90:1–4   **TUESDAY** • Psalm 23:1–6
WEDNESDAY • Psalm 90:12–17
THURSDAY • Psalm 24:1–10   **FRIDAY** • Psalm 150:1–6

Song for the Season

Sing a song of your choice.

Short Verse

READER   The ancient command remains true today: "You shall love the LORD your God with all your heart and with all your soul and with all your might." Deuteronomy 6:5

Short Prayer

READER   Father, bless us as we journey together.

Scripture Reading

EVERYONE   Father, open our eyes that we might see the wonders of your truth.

MONDAY

God made a covenant with Abraham that all families would be blessed by his family: "I will make you into a great nation and I will bless you; I will make your name great, and you will be a blessing." Genesis 12:2 (NIV)

Additional Reading: Genesis 17:1–8

TUESDAY

Joshua proclaimed it to the entire nation: "As for me and my household, we will serve the LORD." Joshua 24:15 (NIV)

Additional Reading: Joshua 24:14–28

WEDNESDAY

Solomon wrote, "Listen, my sons, to a father's instruction; pay attention and gain understanding." Proverbs 4:1 (NIV)

Additional Reading: Proverbs 4:1–13

THURSDAY

God reminded his people: "When you have eaten and are satisfied, praise the LORD your God for the good land he has given you. Be careful that you do not forget the LORD your God." Deuteronomy 8:10–11 (NIV)

Additional Reading: Deuteronomy 8:10–18; Psalm 100

FRIDAY

Every aspect of our lives is wrapped up in the gospel of Jesus Christ: "Whatever you do, whether in word or deed, do it all in the name of the Lord Jesus, giving thanks to God the Father through him." Colossians 3:17 (NIV)

Additional Reading: Deuteronomy 6:4–7, 20–25

Open Intercession or Daily Intercession
For daily intercessions see Appendix F.

Prayer for the Week

Father, enlighten us that we may love all your creation, the whole and every grain of sand in it. May we love every leaf, every ray of your light.

Jesus, illumine us that we might love the animals, love the plants, love all that you have created.

For we believe that if we love everything, then, Holy Spirit, you will allow us to perceive the divine mystery in things. And once we perceive it, we will begin to comprehend it and live more fully every day.

God, teach us to love you and all that you have created. *Amen.* *—Inspired by a passage from Dostoevsky's* The Brothers Karamazov *(chapter 41)*

Song for the Season ✠
Sing a song of your choice.

The Celebration of the Journey

The home gathering for autumn is called *The Celebration of the Journey*. This celebration commemorates the final harvest and the great wedding feast of the Lamb. This celebration is intended to tell the final chapter of God's redemptive story.

This home gathering is an homage to the last great festival in the Scriptures, the Feast of Tabernacles.[72] This ancient festival is the only one of the ancient Hebrew festivals that is yet to be fulfilled. Passover is fulfilled with the death and resurrection of Jesus. Pentecost is fulfilled with the descent of the Holy Spirit. This festival is fulfilled only upon the return of Christ the King.

Overview of *The Celebration of the Journey*

This home gathering spans the longest period of time, from Saturday afternoon to breakfast the next day. Because of its length, this gathering is held on the weekend of the Columbus Day holiday so that individuals and families have time to rest on Sunday and Monday.

Below is the organization for this home gathering:

Afternoon activities

Saturday evening celebratory meal

Community festival

Saturday Afternoon Activities

GAMES FOR ADULTS AND CHILDREN ✛ Games for the afternoon may range from leisurely yard games to more intentional games for the children that help communicate the theme of the season. In addition, those who are planning on camping out overnight may set up their tents during the afternoon.

SETTING UP OF BOOTHS OR TENTS FOR THE FESTIVAL ✛ Individuals or families may set up tailgating tents or a booth for games or foods for the festival. Families or individuals are encouraged to set up a tent where people can come to visit and enjoy a game, music, food, or beverage together. Each booth should also offer space and a chance for people to sit and visit.

Saturday Evening—The Great Feast

BACKGROUND The Saturday evening celebratory meal is called *The Great Feast*. It is designed to embody the wedding feast of the marriage supper of the Lamb. Therefore, the meal should be fine and the mood should be enthusiastic. Also, everyone is encouraged to wear something white to this meal.

PREPARATION Below are the items needed for the liturgy of *The Great Feast*.

Two red candles and one white candle
Palm branch
Fresh fruits and vegetables
Sparkling water
Oil lamps for the table
Bread and oil
Honey
Nice entrée for the meal
Plenty of wine
Champagne or sparkling cider

READERS The host may select the readers prior to the meal.

LITURGY FOR
The Celebration of The Great Feast

The Lighting of the Three Candles

LEADER Tonight we celebrate the dramatic conclusion of the redemptive story. Jesus the bridegroom came and paid a very high price for his bride. He gave his very life. He then betrothed his bride and gave her a precious ring of promise, which is the Holy Spirit. But the bridegroom had to leave to prepare a home for his bride. Now she eagerly awaits his return.

WOMEN I am my beloved's and my beloved is mine.

MEN You are perfectly beautiful, my bride. In you I find no flaw. Your lips are sweet as honey. You love is better than wine.

LEADER   Tonight, we begin by lighting the three candles. The first candle is the candle of faith. It is dark red, representing the faith of our ancestors, like that of Rahab. The second red candle is the candle of hope, where we look forward to the bridegroom's return. And finally, we have the candle of love, representing the unquenchable love of our God for his people.

LEADER   We praise you, God, King of the Universe, for you have given us the light of your love.

A woman lights the three candles.

LEADER   These three remain: faith, hope, and love. Faith will be unnecessary when we see him and are like him. Our hope will be complete when what we have waited for has come. But God's love for us and our love for him will last forever. The greatest of these is love.

The Choice Fruit and the Palm Branch

LEADER   This celebration reaches back to an ancient feast that is thousands of years old. The people of Israel were instructed to set aside their choicest fruits and palm fronds. Tonight we do the same. We wave the palm branch and welcome the return of our King.

If present, children are encouraged to wave the palm branches. If no children are present, the leader may wave the branch.

READER   In the book of Revelation, when the King returns, this is the festival that will be celebrated: "A great multitude that no one could count, from every nation, tribe, people, and language, were standing before the throne and in front of the Lamb. They were wearing white robes and were holding palm branches in their hands. And they cried out in a loud voice: 'Salvation belongs to our God, who sits on the throne, and to the Lamb.'"

The leader encourages the participants to enjoy the fruit.

Song for the Season ✠
Sing a song of your choice.

The Living Water

LEADER   As John the apostle recounts, when Jesus first came to earth and walked among us, he attended this feast. On the last and greatest day of the feast, Jesus stood and said in a loud voice,

READER   "If anyone is thirsty, let him come to me and drink. Whoever believes in me, as the Scripture has said, streams of living water will flow from within them." By this he meant the Spirit, whom those who believed in him were later to receive.

READER[73]   Later tonight we will see this part of the festival. During this festival celebration, the celebrant would pour water on a burning fire. Smoke would rush upward, representing God leading his people by a cloud by day and a pillar of fire by night. This was a symbol of God's Spirit leading his people.

READER   Water would also stream from the altar. This water was a symbol of the great river flowing in the City of God. When God restores all of creation, it is written: "On that day, living water will flow from Jerusalem. The LORD will be king over the whole earth. On that day there will be one LORD, and his name the only name."

READER   Jesus said that not only was he the living water, but that out of those who believe in him, streams of living water will flow, as well. The same Spirit that led the people of God by cloud and flame would flow through the followers of Jesus. We would be his people, his city, his bride. Tonight we drink the sparkling water, a symbol of the living water of Jesus flowing through us.

Everyone drinks the sparkling water.

The Lamp, the Bread, and the Oil

LEADER   Jesus told a parable about the kingdom of heaven and his return for his bride:

READER   "The kingdom of heaven will be like ten virgins who took their lamps and went out to meet the bridegroom. Five of them were foolish and five were wise. The foolish ones took their lamps but did not take any oil with them. The wise, however, took oil in jars along with their lamps. The bridegroom was a long time in coming, and they all became drowsy and fell asleep."

READER   "At midnight the cry rang out: 'Here's the bridegroom! Come out to meet him!' Then all the virgins woke up and trimmed their lamps. The foolish ones said to the wise, 'Give us some of your oil; our lamps are going out.' 'No,' they replied, 'there may not be enough for both us and you. Instead, go to those who sell oil and buy some for yourselves.' But while they were on their way to buy the oil, the bridegroom arrived. The virgins who were ready went in with him to the wedding banquet."

The leader holds up an oil lamp.

LEADER Tonight the table is lit by oil lamps. As God's church, his bride, we state we are ready for the wedding feast. We dip our bread in the olive oil and say:

WOMEN I am my beloved's and my beloved is mine.

Everyone eats dips the bread into the oil.

MEN I have come into my garden, my bride; I have eaten my honeycomb and honey.

WOMEN This is my lover, his mouth is pure and sweet.

Everyone dips the bread into the honey.

The Meal and the Wine

READER O God, you are our God. We exalt you and praise your name, for in perfect faithfulness you have done marvelous things, things planned long ago.

READER You have been a refuge for the poor, a refuge for the needy in his distress, a shelter from the storm, and a shade from the heat.

READER On the Holy Mountain, the place of the City of God, the Lord Almighty will prepare a feast of rich food for all peoples, a banquet of aged wine—the best of meats and the finest of wines.

LEADER We praise you, God, King of the Universe, for this feast—for the food and the wine. We look forward to the Great Feast in the new Jerusalem celebrating you, our King, and your kingdom, which will never end.

Everyone drinks from a cup of wine, and the liturgy pauses for the meal.

Giving Thanks

LEADER God, you promised Abraham that we, his descendants, would inherit a land of promise. And you told us that when we have eaten and are satisfied, we should praise the Lord our God for the good land he has given us.

READER Surely this is our God; we trusted in him, and he saved us. Let us rejoice and be glad in his salvation.

The Bride Prepared for Her Husband

LEADER I saw the Holy City, the new Jerusalem, coming down out of heaven from God, prepared as a bride beautifully dressed for her husband.

MEN The bridegroom says, "Behold, I am coming soon. I am the Alpha and the Omega, the First and the Last, the Beginning and the End."

WOMEN   The Spirit and the bride say, "Come!" And let him who hears say, "Come!"
Whoever is thirsty, let him come; whoever wishes, let him take the
free gift of the water of life.
Everyone drinks the champagne or sparkling cider.

Song for the Season ✟
Sing a song of your choice.

Introducing the Community Festival and the Tents

LEADER   Tonight we will celebrate. As we near the end of this year, we anticipate
the conclusion of God's redemptive plan. We will celebrate the finality ·
of the Great Feast with music, games, and food. As wonderful as this
festival is, we are reminded that we are still journeying toward the
Great City.

READER   By faith Abraham made his home in the promised land like a stranger in
a foreign country; he lived in tents, as did Isaac and Jacob, who were
heirs with him of the same promise. For he was looking forward to the
city with foundations, whose architect and builder is God.

LEADER   The tents outside represent our journey of faith. Just like the grandfather
of our faith, Abraham, we are still journeying toward the City of God.
Let us all find joy in the journey and celebrate the beauty of our faith.

Song for the Season ✟
Sing a song of your choice.

The Beginning of the Festival ✟
*As the evening festival begins, the leader gathers the participants' attention to begin
the festival.*

LEADER   Tonight, we begin our festival with a symbol from the ancient festival.
The leader pours water into the fire (being careful not to extinguish the fire).

READER   Jesus said: "If anyone is thirsty, let him come to me and drink. Whoever
believes in me, as the Scripture has said, streams of living water will
flow from within them."

LEADER   Enjoy the festival!
*Optional campout: If the host so desires, the venue allows, and if the
participants so desire, individuals or families may want to camp out in
tents to continue the theme of the journey.*

Sunday Breakfast or Brunch

The Celebration of the Journey concludes with a celebratory breakfast or brunch.

READER   Glorious things of you are spoken, City of our God.

READER   Singers and dancers will come celebrating, saying, "The springs of life are in you, City of God."

READER   Great is the Lord and greatly to be praised. In the City of our God all is beautiful. Walk around her, consider each portion of the City. See God's beauty everywhere.

READER   Our God reigns forever and ever. The King is enthroned above all, and of his reign there will be no end. *Amen.*

LEADER   Today, we celebrate the conclusion of the Redemptive Story, when the heavenly city descends and God's peaceable Kingdom is fully expressed here on earth.

      This morning, we will eat and drink of oranges, lemons, limes, and grapefruit. In the Scriptures, this holiday calls for the fruit of "splendid trees." These fruits are symbols of celebration and joy. Today, we celebrate God's greatness and how he brings restoration to that which is fallen.

The meal should contain juices and dishes with the above fruits.

LEADER   These fruits also remind us of the Tree of Life.

READER   The Tree of Life will yield twelve kinds of fruit, one each month. And the leaves of the tree are for the healing of all nations.

READER   There will be a day when there will be no cold or frost. Living waters will flow out of God's City, and the Lord will be King over all the earth. And the city will have no need of sun or moon to shine on it, for the glory of God gives it light.

READER   All nations will come together and find their citizenship in Zion, the glorious City of God.

All participants stand, form a circle around the table, and sing.

Song of Celebration ✠
Sing a song of your choice.

Appendices

APPENDIX A Definitions and Colors for Each Season

ADVENT	Royal blue	First four weeks of the liturgical year
CHRISTMAS	Red and green	Two weeks of Christmas
EPIPHANY	White or gold	Four weeks following two weeks of Christmas
WINTER ORDINARY	Green or light blue	From February to Ash Wednesday
LENT	Purple or lavender	Ash Wednesday to Easter Sunday
EASTER TO PENTECOST	White or gold	Easter to Pentecost Sunday
AFTER PENTECOST	Red	Pentecost Sunday to the end of June
SUMMER ORDINARY	Green or light green	First of July to the end of August
AUTUMN ORDINARY	Green or dark red	September through the end of the liturgical year

APPENDIX B Essential Dates of the Liturgical Calendar

ADVENT TO EASTER

	winter					*spring*	
	ADVENT BEGINS * **	CHRISTMAS DAY 12/25 *	EPIPHANY DAY 1/06	CELEBRATION OF THE KING	FIRST SABBATH OF ORDINARY TIME **	ASH WEDNESDAY	EASTER
			Introduction on Page 15.			*Introduction on Page 81.*	
2011	NOV 28	SAT.	THURS.	JAN 08	FEB 06	MAR 09	APR 24
2012	NOV 27	SUN.	FRI.	JAN 07	FEB 05	FEB 22	APR 08
2013	DEC 02	TUES.	SUN.	JAN 05	FEB 03	FEB 13	MAR 31
2014	DEC 01	WED.	MON.	JAN 11	FEB 09	MAR 05	APR 20
2015	NOV 30	THURS.	TUES.	JAN 10	FEB 08	FEB 18	APR 05
2016	NOV 29	FRI.	WED.	JAN 09	FEB 07	FEB 10	MAR 27
2017	NOV 27	SUN.	FRI.	JAN 07	FEB 05	MAR 01	APR 16
2018	DEC 03	MON.	SAT.	JAN 06	FEB 04	FEB 14	APR 01
2019	DEC 02	TUES.	SUN.	JAN 05	FEB 03	MAR 06	APR 21
2020	DEC 01	WED.	MON.	JAN 11	FEB 09	FEB 26	APR 12
2021	NOV 29	FRI.	WED.	JAN 09	FEB 07	FEB 17	APR 04
2022	NOV 28	SAT.	THURS.	JAN 08	FEB 06	MAR 02	APR 17
2023	NOV 27	SUN.	FRI.	JAN 07	FEB 05	FEB 22	APR 09
2024	DEC 03	MON.	SAT.	JAN 06	FEB 04	FEB 14	MAR 31
2025	DEC 01	WED.	MON.	JAN 11	FEB 09	MAR 05	APR 20
2026	NOV 30	THURS.	TUES.	JAN 10	FEB 08	FEB 18	APR 05
2027	NOV 29	FRI.	WED.	JAN 09	FEB 07	FEB 10	MAR 28
2028	NOV 28	SAT.	THURS.	JAN 08	FEB 06	MAR 01	APR 16
2029	DEC 03	MON.	SAT.	JAN 06	FEB 04	FEB 14	APR 01
2030	DEC 02	TUES.	SUN.	JAN 05	FEB 03	MAR 06	APR 21

* In the calendar year 2010, but liturgical year 2011.
** The Sabbath liturgy begins the Saturday night prior to this Sunday.

APPENDIX C Essential Dates of the Liturgical Calendar
PENTECOST THROUGH THE END OF THE YEAR

	summer		*autumn*		
	PENTECOST SUNDAY (TIME OF THE CHURCH)	FIRST SABBATH OF ORDINARY TIME** (TIME OF THE KINGDOM)	FIRST SABBATH OF ORDINARY TIME (TIME OF THE JOURNEY)	DAY OF REPENTANCE	CELEBRATION OF THE JOURNEY
	Introduction on Page 141		*Introduction on Page 195*		
2011	JUN 12	JUL 03	AUG 28	SEP 18	OCT 11
2012	MAY 27	JUL 01	SEP 02	OCT 08	OCT 08
2013	MAY 19	JUL 07	SEP 01	SEP 26	OCT 14
2014	JUN 08	JUL 06	AUG 31	SEP 14	OCT 13
2015	MAY 24	JUL 05	AUG 30	OCT 04	OCT 12
2016	MAY 15	JUL 03	AUG 28	SEP 23	OCT 10
2017	JUN 04	JUL 02	SEP 03	OCT 12	OCT 09
2018	MAY 20	JUL 01	SEP 02	SEP 30	OCT 08
2019	JUN 09	JUL 07	SEP 01	SEP 19	OCT 14
2020	MAY 31	JUL 05	AUG 30	OCT 09	OCT 12
2021	MAY 23	JUL 04	AUG 29	SEP 28	OCT 11
2022	JUN 05	JUL 03	AUG 28	SEP 16	OCT 10
2023	MAY 28	JUL 02	SEP 03	OCT 05	OCT 09
2024	MAY 19	JUL 07	SEP 01	SEP 25	OCT 14
2025	JUN 08	JUL 06	AUG 31	OCT 12	OCT 13
2026	MAY 24	JUL 05	AUG 30	OCT 02	OCT 12
2027	MAY 16	JUL 04	AUG 29	SEP 21	OCT 11
2028	JUN 04	JUL 02	SEP 03	OCT 11	OCT 09
2029	MAY 20	JUL 01	SEP 02	SEP 30	OCT 08
2030	JUN 09	JUL 07	SEP 01	SEP 19	OCT 14

** *The Sabbath liturgy begins the Saturday night prior to this Sunday.*

Those who would like their homes to be blessed by other families may invite a few families together for a simple dinner or for coffee.

The Lighting of the Candle

LEADER   Most High God, may your blessing come to rest on this home. Make the lives of those in this home wise with your wisdom. As we light this candle, kindle in our hearts the fire of your love, and may your Word made flesh make his home among us.

LEADER   The peace of Christ be upon this house.

EVERYONE   And to all who live here.

A Psalm

READER   Unless the LORD builds the house,
     those who build it labor in vain.
Unless the LORD watches over the city,
     the watchman stays awake in vain.
It is in vain that you rise up early
     and go late to rest,
eating the bread of anxious toil;
     for he gives to his beloved sleep.
Behold, children are a heritage from the LORD,
     the fruit of the womb a reward.
Like arrows in the hand of a warrior
     are the children of one's youth.
Blessed is the man
     who fills his quiver with them!
He shall not be put to shame
     when he speaks with his enemies in the gate.
—*Psalm 127*

Instead of Psalm 127, Psalm 3 may be used

You, O LORD, are a shield about me,
     my glory, and the lifter of my head.
I cried aloud to the LORD,
     and he answered me from his holy hill.

I lay down and slept;
   I woke again, for the LORD sustained me.
Arise, O LORD!
   Save me, O my God!
Salvation belongs to the LORD;
   your blessing be on your people!
   —*Psalm* 3:3–5, 7–8

Song for the Season ✠

Sing a song of your choice.

At the Entrance of the Home

May God pour out his blessing on all who live here.
The peace of Christ be on this home from roof to floor
From wall to wall,
From end to end,
From its foundation and in its covering.
In the strong name of the Father, Son, and Holy Spirit
May all evil be banished,
May all oppression and confusion be removed,
May all strife cease,
So that God's Spirit alone might dwell here
And bring this home peace.
   —*Inspired by a home blessing prayer of the Northumbria Community*

A Commitment of the Home

READER   Joshua said to the people, "The LORD, the God of Israel, says, 'Long ago, your fathers served other gods. But I took your father Abraham and led him to a new land and gave him a promise and a great lineage. I gave him Isaac, Jacob, and Esau. I sent Moses and Aaron, and I brought you out of slavery from the land of Egypt.

   "'The Egyptians pursued your fathers with chariots and horsemen to the Red Sea. And when they cried to the LORD, God put darkness between you and the Egyptians and made the sea come upon them and cover them; and your eyes saw what he did in Egypt. You lived in the wilderness a long time. But then God brought you to the land he promised. Enemies fought with you, and God gave them into your hand, and you took possession of their land. Enemies tried to curse you but God stopped them. Instead, God made your enemies bless you. He delivered you once again.

"'And then you crossed the Jordan and came to Jericho, and still encountered much resistance. And God gave your enemies into your hand. Today, you eat the fruit of vineyards and olive orchards that you did not plant.'"

"Now fear and love the LORD and serve him in sincerity and in faithfulness. Put away the false gods that you served beyond the River and in Egypt, and serve the LORD. Choose this day whom you will serve, whether the gods your fathers Abraham, Isaac, and Jacob served, or the gods of the people in whose land you dwell. As for me and my house, we will serve the LORD."

—Adapted from Joshua 24

EVERYONE   As for me and my house, we will serve the LORD.

LEADER   Make this house a place of peace for this family and a place of warmth and caring for all our friends. Loving God, enlighten us with your presence, so that, as we go into the world, we might clearly see our way to you and discover you in our work, in our school, and in all our endeavors. This we ask to your glory and in the power of your kingship.

EVERYONE   May your kingdom come and your will be done in this home as it is in heaven. For yours is the kingdom and the power and the glory now and forever. *Amen.*

LEADER   The peace of Christ above all; peace on this home.
Christ be the life of all who live within this place.
May he provide strength and comfort to all.
And may he grant light and joy.
May the peace of Christ rule in our hearts and
May the word of Christ in all its richness dwell in us,
So that whatever is done in this home, in word or in deed,
Will be done in the name of the Lord.

Father, we bless this home in the name of the Father, the Son, and the Holy Spirit.

The people may make the sign of the cross as the leader concludes.

244

LEADER   An ancient tradition of the faith is the anointing of the home. The sweet fragrance is a sign of God's presence and his peace. When Jesus visited his dear friends Mary, Martha, and Lazarus, Mary anointed Jesus' feet, and the fragrance filled the house. May the fragrance of the peace of Christ fill this house both now and forever.

The leader may pour the aromatic oil into a fragrance diffuser.

Blessing of the Home

LEADER   May the peace of the Lord Christ go with you, wherever his Spirit may lead you. May he guide you through the wilderness and protect you through the storm. May he bring you home rejoicing at the wonders he has shown you. May he bring you home rejoicing once again into the doors of this house. In the name of the Father, and of the Son, and of the Holy Spirit. *Amen.*

—Based on prayers of the Northumbria Community

After the brief liturgy, the families may enjoy coffee or light refreshments.

AN ANCIENT YET FRESH APPROACH TO THE SCRIPTURES

A working definition for *Midrash* could be this: "a dynamic community dialogue focused on the text of the Scriptures that intends to bring out or search out both its ancient and present meanings." Professor of Judaic Studies Jacob Neusner, however, said it more simply, "Midrash starts with Scripture and ends with community."[74] Many would argue that the New Testament and even Jesus' approach to teaching contain Midrashic elements. Jesus was a master at asking piercing questions that reached to the heart of the scriptural matter in question while simultaneously getting to the heart of the reader.

The intent of this Midrashic approach is not to elicit an outpouring of personal sentiments, though it does engage the personal. A good Midrash engages a person as a whole person, dealing with many layers—the intellectual, the poetic, the relational, and the emotional, just to name a few. It should both engage and challenge the beliefs of the readers/listeners/conversers, constantly pushing them to wrestle with the text. Midrash believes that discovery and even transformation takes place in the struggle with the Scriptures themselves.

The struggle with the text, however, cannot be isolated. It requires a community of interpreters stimulating and challenging each other. In the process of the conversation, the community submits to and depends on each other, realizing a transformation not only of the individual, but also of the relationships within the community. In Midrash the Spirit awakens the different gifts of the body of Christ, allowing many voices to speak as one.

Below are a few guidelines to create an insightful Midrashic discussion:

1 READ THE TEXT ALOUD. Reading the text aloud allows the participants to receive the text through another medium besides reading it silently to themselves. Hearing and reading are different ways of engaging with the text. Both are helpful, even necessary.

2 STAY FOCUSED ON THE TEXT AT HAND. An important characteristic of Midrash is that it stays focused on the Scripture at hand. Midrash is a great equalizer. People with deep scriptural backgrounds and those who are new to the text are equally important within the context of a good Midrash.

. This dialogue should not support one individual's interpretation or disposition toward the text. Rather, the leader needs to keep all participants coming back to the text. Midrash is like singing in a chorus or playing with a band or an ensemble. Each voice is necessary, but one voice cannot be dominant.

3 A GOOD LEADER IS INTEGRAL TO GOOD MIDRASH. The leader of the dialogue should be like a director or conductor, rather than a virtuoso musician. A good Midrash leader does not like to give answers, but rather asks questions that support the participants as they explore. The leader is a guide through the discussion and the Scriptures.

If you don't know how to lead a Midrash discussion, the best way to learn is to try. Don't be daunted by the task. The scriptural text will do the work; it's been the subject of vibrant conversation for thousands of years.

4 THE LEADER SHOULD USE THE FIRST QUESTION TO ENGAGE THE CONVERSERS AND DRAW OUT THEIR IMMEDIATE RESPONSES. The first question should be extremely open-ended. A good leading question could be, "What stood out to you?" or, "What are your first thoughts or first response to this text?" This may seem self-evident, but the first open-ended question welcomes the participants and establishes the leader as a guide through the conversation, rather than the source of information.

5 WHEN THE CONVERSATION STRAYS, THE LEADER SHOULD DIRECT THE CONVERSATION BACK TO THE TEXT. As participants respond, the leader must continually direct them back to the text. When someone asks a question, the leader may respond with, "What does the text say?" Though biblical insight provides an important layer that deepens the conversation, it is important that the "biblically educated" do not dominate the discussion. Again, the voice of the biblical scholar is an extremely important voice, but it is not the only voice. The leader should always point the conversation back to the text. Not only does it keep everyone on a level playing field, but also it values the practical authority of the text over one person's ideas.

6 FOCUS ON THE PECULIAR OR THE DISTINCTIVE. In discussing the text, help the participants pay attention to details that might get overlooked. For example, on the road to Emmaus in Luke 24, when Jesus is talking with the two men and they ask him if he has heard about the things that have transpired over the weekend, Jesus responds, "What things?" Of course, Jesus knows what they are talking about. He was the center of the entire event. But Jesus is doing something important for those he is teaching. Pointing out these types of details not only highlights the cleverness of the text, but also starts to steer participants toward the type of teaching Jesus is doing in the passage.

7 CONCLUDE WITH THE BIG PICTURE. Many times the conversation may get focused or even bogged down on the details. The leader may redirect the conversation by asking questions such as, "What do you think the big point of this text is?" or, "What does this text tell us about God?" or, "What does this text tell us about ourselves?" or, "What are the major assumptions behind this text?"

Overall, Midrash will stimulate different reactions from different readers. For some it will catalyze imaginative expression. For others it will pique intellectual curiosity. The point of the discussion is to intertwine the participants with the Scriptures and with each other. The differing points of view and dispositions are necessary for a fuller, richer expression of the body of Christ.

Finally, a Midrashic discourse believes that the Scriptures are necessary for the community and the community necessary for the Scriptures. The process may yield complex results, but community is like that. Good, rich community does not produce a homogenized product. Rather, community is like fine wine, filled with complexities that include both subtleties and intriguing imperfections.

248

APPENDIX F Intercessions for Each Weekday

Below are some guidelines and common prayers for weekday intercessory prayers.

Beginning the Time of Open Intercession

LEADER Our Father, we lift up our dear friends and family.

We ask your grace and blessings on _____.

Family members speak the names of the friends and family members for whom they wish to intercede.

MONDAY—INTERCESSION FOR THE FAMILY

Each family member may pray for the family member that sits next to him or her.

LEADER Our Father, you created us for a peaceful, loving relationship with you and each other. We pray this home will be a place of your peace. We lift our hearts to you in thankfulness for the love you have for our family. Bless us with mutual submission and understanding for each other. Help us to consider each other above ourselves. Our loving Father, may our love for each other bless you and those who enter this house. May you incarnate your love and demonstrate your glory to all who enter in this home. *Amen.*
—*Based on a prayer from the Hebrew Siddur*

TUESDAY—INTERCESSION FOR THOSE WHO OFFEND US

Family members silently ask God to forgive those who have sinned against them and those who currently act as enemies. Also, we ask for forgiveness for any harm or wrong we have caused to others.

LEADER Lord Jesus Christ, you commanded us to love our enemies and those who injure us. Instead of holding onto anger or bitterness, tonight we choose to pray for them and forgive them. In the moment of your greatest pain, you prayed for your enemies, that our Father would forgive those who chose to crucify you. Grant us, we pray, the spirit and ministry of reconciliation that we may forgive any and every pain and be reconciled with our enemies. Grant us to overcome offenses with humility and the true love of those we encounter. We ask you, Lord, to give to our enemies mercy, true peace, and forgiveness of sins; and do not allow them to leave this life without faith. And help us to repay evil with goodness, and to remain safe from the temptations of our adversary and from all that threatens us, in the form of visible and invisible enemies. *Amen.* —*Based on a traditional Eastern Orthodox prayer*

WEDNESDAY—INTERCESSION FOR THE COMMUNITY

LEADER   Our Father, we pray for this community of faith, this family of families, with whom we share life. Protect our marriages and make them flourish. Give husbands great vision, tempered with gentleness and sacrificial love. Give wives liberty, ingenuity, love, and respect. Give wisdom and guidance to fathers and mothers, that we may leave a legacy for our families and pass down the faith of our fathers to our children and grandchildren. And finally, Father, bless our children. Fill them with purpose, so they may live lives worthy of the calling that you have placed on them. Give them hearts that long to love you, minds that long to know you, and spirits that long to follow you. Bless our families in this community, that the kingdom of God may rise among us. *Amen.*

THURSDAY—INTERCESSION FOR THE CITY OR REGION WHERE WE LIVE

LEADER   Our Father, who art in heaven, hallowed be your name. Your kingdom come, your will be done in *[the city or region where you live]* as it is in heaven. Give us this day our daily bread and forgive us our sins, as we forgive those who sin against us. And lead us not into temptation, but deliver us from evil. For yours is the kingdom, and the power, and the glory, forever and ever. *Amen.*

FRIDAY—INTERCESSION FOR THE OPPRESSED AND THE PERSECUTED

LEADER   Father, we remember those who are oppressed and those who suffer for your sake.

Family members remain silent as we remember those who sacrifice their lives for the gospel.

LEADER   Almighty and everlasting God, hear the cries of the oppressed and the cries of your people as we call to you for your persecuted church throughout the world, those who know the fellowship of sharing in your sufferings. As you heard the cries of your ancient people in bondage in Egypt and came down to deliver them, so now listen to the suffering of the persecuted church in our time. Give bread to those who are hungry, comfort to the imprisoned, strength to the tortured, and all for the sake of Jesus, who lived and died for us, who now lives and reigns with you and the Holy Spirit, one God, forever and ever. —*Based on a prayer of Rev. Dr. Grant LeMarquand*

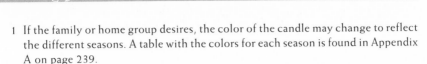

Notes

1 If the family or home group desires, the color of the candle may change to reflect the different seasons. A table with the colors for each season is found in Appendix A on page 239.

2 The family may share one cup or, for hygienic purposes, may pour multiple cups.

3 Families or home groups may want to either buy a special loaf of bread or take the time to bake a loaf of bread themselves.

4 For dates for *The Celebration of the King* see the table in Appendix B on page 239 or the athomewithgod.org website.

5 The Jesse tree project is simply the use of canvases or other crafts rather than decorating a separate tree.

6 The candle color for Advent is purple or royal blue, symbolizing Christ, the coming King. Some churches replace one purple candle with a pink one, representing the joy of the Virgin Mary as she prepared to give birth to the Christ child.

7 For all of the liturgies in this book, parents may encourage their children's participation by asking the children to read or by helping them read the verses (if the child cannot read). Older groups may want to read the longer passages listed in the Additional Reading.

8 For additional information on leading a dynamic discussion over the Scriptures, see the explanation and tutorial given in Appendix E on page 245.

9 Depending on the liturgical dates for this year, this Sabbath liturgy may or may not be necessary. See Appendix B or the athomewithgod.org website for exact dates for the season. Because the Sabbaths and weekday liturgies for Epiphany always follow immediately after the dates for *The Celebration of the King*, in certain years this liturgy will be unnecessary.

10 The Hebrew word *Bethlehem* may be translated as the "house of bread."

11 See the note above about the dates for the season in the Opening Sabbath liturgy.

12 The leader may wish to review the table for the dates of the season in Appendix B to determine which weekend transitions to the Sabbath for the Lenten season.

13 Ordinary seasons are usually represented by the color green; however, families may wish to use alternative colors during the ordinary seasons.

14 This Sabbath falls on the first weekend of February.

15 Depending on the liturgical dates for this year, these Sabbath liturgies may or may not be necessary. If Ash Wednesday occurred before this Sabbath, then the liturgies for Lent should be used. For each year's Lenten dates, see Appendix B or register with the athomewithgod.org website to receive seasonal and date reminders.

16 This Sabbath falls on the first weekend of February.

17 See the note above about the dates for the Lenten season. If Ash Wednesday occurred before this Sabbath, or any of the following Sabbaths, then the liturgies for Lent should be used.

18 The candle color for Advent is purple or royal blue, symbolizing Christ, the coming King. Some churches replace one purple candle with a pink one, representing the joy of the Virgin Mary as she prepared to give birth to the Christ child.

19 Parents of young children can encourage their children's participation by making this time of meditation more physical by incorporating a series of stretches set

to calming music. See the athomewithgod.org website for more information and ideas for weekday prayer and worship.

20 This intermediary week usually occurs the first week of February. For exact dates for the beginning of this season, see the table in Appendix B.

21 The color for the Winter Ordinary Time is green or light blue.

22 See Appendix B or the athomewithgod.org website for the dates for Lent.

23 See Appendix B or the athomewithgod.org website for the dates for Lent.

24 See Appendix B or the athomewithgod.org website for the dates for Lent.

25 See Appendix B or the athomewithgod.org website for the dates for Lent.

26 Salmon is preferable for the fish entrée. It represents the countercultural essence of the faith, "swimming upstream" against the current of present-day culture.

27 A King's Cake is a traditional dessert for Epiphany representing the attendant Three Kings and also Jesus' kingship. A recipe for King's Cake may be found on the athomewithgod.org website.

28 Numerous sticks may be hidden so that all children can find a scavenger hunt item.

29 Based on words of St. Gregory of Nazianzus.

30 Based on a prayer of the *Book of Common Prayer*, 1928.

31 A coffee cake or yellow cake can be used if a King's Cake cannot be purchased or made.

32 In the early church, Passover and Easter were the same holiday. Not until much later were the two holidays made distinct. For more on the history of Passover and Easter in the early church, see the athomewithgod.org website.

33 The first Sabbath for the Lenten season begins *after* Ash Wednesday.

34 The color for the Lenten season is purple or lavender.

35 This Sabbath is the beginning of the first full week of Lent. Ash Wednesday begins the season, and the first Sabbath of this season occurs *after* Ash Wednesday.

36 Based on a prayer of St. Ignatius of Loyola.

37 This and the following are based on a prayer of St. Benedict.

38 The color from Easter to Pentecost is white.

39 This color of the candle for this season is purple or lavender.

40 Parents with children can encourage their children's participation by making this time of meditation more physical and incorporating a series of stretches set to calming music. See the athomewithgod.org website for more information and ideas for weekday prayer and worship.

41 Based on a prayer of St. Ignatius of Loyola.

42 The color of the candle for this season is white, representing the risen Christ. The candle (and cross) used on Easter Sunday may be used during this season until Pentecost.

43 The color of the candle for this season is white, representing the risen Christ. The candle (and cross) used on Easter Sunday may be used during this season until Pentecost.

44 For exact dates for the beginning of the season, see Appendix C.

45 The color of the candle for this season is red, a symbol of the fire of the Holy Spirit.

46 Depending on the liturgical dates for this year, the Sabbath liturgies for the third through seventh weeks following Pentecost may or may not be necessary. The weeks following Pentecost are intermediary weeks between Pentecost and the first weekend of July. If the first of July falls on the weekend of the Sabbath's observance, use the Sabbath liturgy for the Time of the Church located on

page 143. For each year's dates, see the table in Appendix C or register on the athomewithgod.org website to receive seasonal and date reminders.

47 See the note about Passover and the intermediary weeks—the third through seventh weeks following Pentecost—in the Opening Sabbath liturgy above.

48 The Time of the Kingdom lasts from the first weekend of July to the end of August.

49 The color of the candle for this season is green or light green, representing new life.

50 This Sabbath always falls on the first weekend of July. See Appendix C or the athomewithgod.org website for exact dates.

51 Depending on the liturgical dates for this year, this Sabbath liturgy may or may not be necessary. See Appendix C or the athomewithgod.org website for exact dates for the season.

52 This Sabbath always falls on the first weekend of July. See Appendix C or the athomewithgod.org website for exact dates.

53 See note about the dates for the season in the Opening Sabbath liturgy above.

54 Parents with young children can encourage their children's participation by making this time of meditation more physical by incorporating a series of stretches set to calming music. See the athomewithgod.org website for more information and ideas for weekday prayer and worship.

55 See Appendix C or the athomewithgod.org website for the dates for the Time of the Kingdom.

56 See Appendix C or the athomewithgod.org website for the dates for the Time of the Kingdom.

57 See Appendix C or the athomewithgod.org website for the dates for the Time of the Kingdom.

58 This season always begins on the first weekend of July. For exact dates for the beginning of this season, see Appendix C.

59 The color of the candle for this season is green, a symbol of new life.

60 The family or home group may prepare an entrée of their choice.

61 The parts for "Reader" in this liturgy should be read by various readers, if possible.

62 This text is a synopsis of Jeremiah 31:33.

63 This text is a synopsis of Ezekiel 37:11–14, 24–28

64 From *Celtic Daily Prayer: Prayers and Readings of the Northumbria Community* (New York: HarperOne, 2002).

65 Based on Psalm 133.

66 A synopsis of 2 Corinthians 3:7–18 and Hebrews 12:18–24.

67 The Time of the Journey begins either the last weekend of August or the first weekend of September, depending on the year. See Appendix C or the athomewithgod.org website for details.

68 The color of the candle for this season is green. Dark red, representing the faith of Rahab, may also be used.

69 For exact dates for the beginning of this season, see Appendix C.

70 The traditional color for this season is green. Dark red, however, may also be used to represent the ancestors of our faith. Dark red is the color of the rope or thread that Rahab placed outside her window, demonstrating her faith in God.

71 Parents with young children can encourage their children's participation by making this time of meditation more physical by incorporating a series of stretches set

to calming music. See the athomewithgod.org website for more information and ideas for weekday prayer and worship.

72 For more information on the theological significance of the Festival of the Tabernacles see the athomewithgod.org website.

73 The parts for "Reader" in this liturgy should be read by various readers, if possible.

74 Jacob Neusner, *What is Midrash? and A Midrash Reader* (Atlanta: Scholars Press, 1994), 9–10.

About Paraclete Press

Who We Are

Paraclete Press is a publisher of books, recordings, and DVDs on Christian spirituality. Our publishing represents a full expression of Christian belief and practice—from Catholic to Evangelical, from Protestant to Orthodox.

We are the publishing arm of the Community of Jesus, an ecumenical monastic community in the Benedictine tradition. As such, we are uniquely positioned in the marketplace without connection to a large corporation and with informal relationships to many branches and denominations of faith.

What We Are Doing

BOOKS Paraclete publishes books that show the richness and depth of what it means to be Christian. Although Benedictine spirituality is at the heart of all that we do, we publish books that reflect the Christian experience across many cultures, time periods, and houses of worship. We publish books that nourish the vibrant life of the church and its people—books about spiritual practice, formation, history, ideas, and customs.

We have several different series, including the best-selling Paraclete Essentials, and Paraclete Giants series of classic texts in contemporary English; A Voice from the Monastery—men and women monastics writing about living a spiritual life today; award-winning literary faith fiction and poetry; and the Active Prayer Series that brings creativity and liveliness to any life of prayer.

RECORDINGS From Gregorian chant to contemporary American choral works, our music recordings celebrate sacred choral music through the centuries. Paraclete distributes the recordings of the internationally acclaimed choir Gloriæ Dei Cantores, praised for their "rapt and fathomless spiritual intensity" by *American Record Guide,* and the Gloriæ Dei Cantores Schola, which specializes in the study and performance of Gregorian chant. Paraclete is also the exclusive North American distributor of the recordings of the Monastic Choir of St. Peter's Abbey in Solesmes, France, long considered to be a leading authority on Gregorian chant.

DVDS Our DVDs offer spiritual help, healing, and biblical guidance for life issues: grief and loss, marriage, forgiveness, anger management, facing death, and spiritual formation.

LEARN MORE ABOUT US AT OUR WEBSITE:
WWW.PARACLETEPRESS.COM, OR CALL US TOLL-FREE AT 1-800-451-5006.

You may also be interested in...

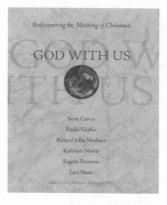

God With Us
Rediscovering the Meaning of Christmas

ISBN: 978-1-55725-541-9 $29.95, HARDCOVER

God With Us is a companion for those who want to experience Christmas as the early Christians once did, set in the larger context of Advent and Epiphany. Through daily meditations, Scripture, prayer, illuminating history and fine art, we experience what saints have glimpsed through the ages—the wonder of God made flesh.

Contributors: Scott Cairns, Emilie Griffin, Richard John Neuhaus, Kathleen Norris, Eugene Peterson, Luci Shaw
EDITED BY GREG PENNOYER AND GREGORY WOLFE

The Paraclete Psalter

ISBN: 978-1-55725-663-8 $24.99, BONDED LEATHER

It was common practice among the early Christians to pray the entire Book of Psalms each month. This simple, easy-to-follow book, featuring the NIV text, will guide you through the entire Psalter every four weeks. You will come to know God as Friend, Shepherd, Defender, Father, Provider, Savior, and Lord, as you pray these words, allowing them to enter into your heart and life through faithful repetition.